HOTSPOTS
BARBA

KT-429-799

Thomas Cook

Written by Skye Hernandez
Original photography by Skye Hernandez

Published by Thomas Cook Publishing
A division of Thomas Cook Tour Operations Limited.
Company Registration no. 3772199 England
The Thomas Cook Business Park, Unit 9, Coningsby Road,
Peterborough PE3 8SB, United Kingdom
Email: books@thomascook.com, Tel: + 44 (0) 1733 416477
www.thomascookpublishing.com

Produced by Cambridge Publishing Management Limited
Burr Elm Court, Main Street, Caldecote CB23 7NU

ISBN: 978-1-84848-179-4

First edition © 2009 Thomas Cook Publishing
Text © Thomas Cook Publishing
Maps © Thomas Cook Publishing/PCGraphics (UK) Limited

Series Editor: Adam Royal
Production/DTP: Steven Collins

Printed and bound in Spain by GraphyCems

Cover photography: 4Corners/Fantuz Olimpio

CONTENTS

WHAT'S IN YOUR GUIDEBOOK?

Independent authors Impartial up-to-date information from our travel experts who meticulously source local knowledge.

Experience Thomas Cook's 165 years in the travel industry and guidebook publishing enriches every word with expertise you can trust.

Travel know-how Thomas Cook has thousands of staff working around the globe, all living and breathing travel.

Editors Travel-publishing professionals, pulling everything together to craft a perfect blend of words, pictures, maps and design.

You, the traveller We deliver a practical, no-nonsense approach to information, geared to how you really use it.

ABOUT THE AUTHOR

Skye Hernandez is a Trinidadian writer and editor. She has been a journalist for many years and has worked with the island's major newspapers and in broadcast media. She is a former managing editor of *Caribbean Beat* and *MACO Caribbean Living* magazines. She holds a BA degree in Latin American Studies from the University of Toronto, Canada.

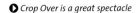

● *Crop Over is a great spectacle*

INTRODUCTION
Getting to know Barbados

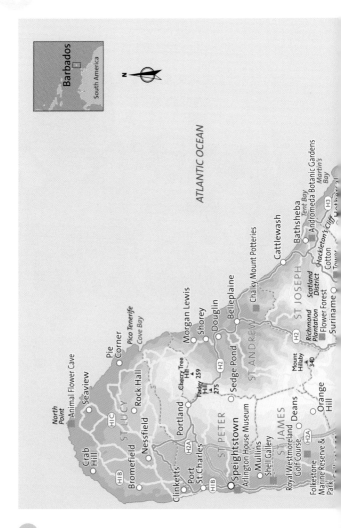

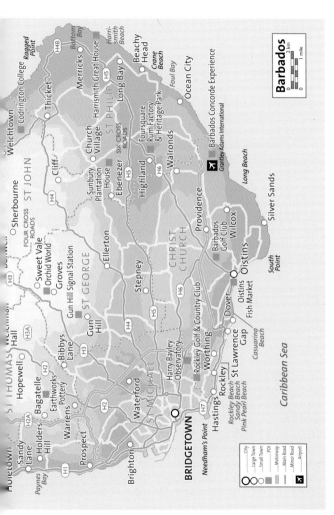

Barbados

0 — 2 km
0 — 1 mile

Ragged Point
H8
Bottom Bay
Harrismith Beach
Beachy Head
Crane Beach
Foul Bay
Ocean City
Barbados Concorde Experience
Grantley Adams International
Long Beach
Silver Sands
South Point

Codrington College
Welchtown
Thicket
Merricks
Harrismith Great House H5
Long Bay
Sherbourne
Cliff
H4
Church Village
ST PHILIP
SIX CROSS ROADS
Sunbury Plantation House
Ebenezer H5
Foursquare Rum Factory & Heritage Park
Highland H6
Walronds
Providence
Wilcox
Barbados Golf Club
Oistins
Oistins Fish Market
ST JOHN
FOUR CROSS ROADS
ST GEORGE
Sweet Vale
Orchid World
Groves
Gun Hill Signal Station
Ellerton
Stepney
H5
CHRIST CHURCH
H6
H4
Dover
Gun Hill
Harry Bayley Observatory
Rockley Golf & Country Club
Worthing
St Lawrence Gap
Casuarina Beach
Caribbean Sea

ST THOMAS
Hopewell
Bagatelle H2
Earthworks Pottery
Bibbys Lane
Warrens
Prospect
H3
H3A
Hall
Sandy Lane
Holders Hill
Paynes Bay
H1
Waterford
H2
Brighton
ST MICHAEL
Needham's Point
Hastings
Rockley
H7
Rockley Beach
Sandy Beach
Pink Pearl Beach
BRIDGETOWN

City
Large Town
Small Town
POI
Motorway
Main Road
Minor Road
Airport

7

Getting to know Barbados

Barbados is a breathtakingly beautiful island, a Caribbean dream of amazing beaches, warm turquoise water, rolling sugar cane lands and surprisingly lush forested gullies. The friendly Barbadians, or Bajans as they are familiarly called, seem to genuinely enjoy interacting with visitors and they are proud of their reputation for excellent service. They are a hard-working, conservative and religious people, but as their Crop Over festivities show (see page 105) they also know how to 'wuk up' (a frenetic waist-rotating dance) and have a good time.

Barbados is the easternmost island of the Caribbean, the only coral island in the Antillean chain. The capital, Bridgetown, is its only city, and is situated in the southwest of the island. The southern and western beaches have the palest sand and calmest waters, and this is where most of the tourism development is concentrated, with everything from fabulously expensive resorts to modest apartment hotels. The wilder eastern side of the island features spectacular scenery and beaches more suited to long walks than swimming. Here, the Atlantic's feisty waters make for perfect surfing conditions, with Bathsheba the island's surfing mecca. The country is divided into 11 parishes and Barbadians do tend to use the parish names, so it's a good idea to know them.

The island is fortunate in its natural beauty, and the government recognised early on that building a tourism industry was important for its prosperity. Their efforts, over many years, to convert their resources into a viable tourist industry have paid off, and Barbados is one of the safest and most pleasant places for a truly enjoyable holiday. Barbados' long association with Britain (its only colonial ruler from the time it was claimed for King James in 1625 to autonomy in 1961 and full independence in 1966) has been said to have contributed to the island's stability, and its institutions and government are exemplary in the region. There is some underlying tension over its reputation as being 'Little England' but the African heritage of the majority of its population is dominant and Bajans are proud of their culture as Caribbean people. Barbados has always attracted wealthy celebrity guests seeking relaxation and privacy, and the succession of well-heeled visitors seems to grow every year, among them former British Prime Minister Tony Blair and his family, Tiger Woods (whose wedding took place at Sandy Lane Golf Club), the Beckhams, the Clintons and Mick Jagger. But the island is also a treat for those on a much smaller budget, with numerous beach and apartment hotels ensuring you have a great time.

▲ *Bridgetown, the capital of Barbados*

THE BEST OF BARBADOS

Barbados is a tiny island, but its history and culture, nightlife, shopping, its unique geography and the stability of its government make it a treasure.

TOP 10 ATTRACTIONS

- **Harrison's Cave** is a massive underground complex of natural limestone caves and waterfalls, and rightfully Barbados' most popular attraction (see page 87).

- **Atlantis Submarines** take you on a real submarine journey below Barbados' rich undersea world (see page 100).

- **Barbados Museum** is housed in a former military prison in the historic Garrison area. This is the most extensive of several excellent museums in Barbados (see pages 15–16).

- **St Lawrence Gap** is the best place for nightlife on the island, with restaurants, bars and clubs all clustered in one area on the south coast (see pages 43–5).

- **Crane beach** has been called the most romantic beach on the island, and the Crane is indeed one of the most picturesque, peaceful stretches of sand and ocean imaginable (see page 70).

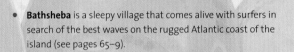

- **Bathsheba** is a sleepy village that comes alive with surfers in search of the best waves on the rugged Atlantic coast of the island (see pages 65–9).

- **Aerial Trek** is an exciting new adventure attraction that gets you gliding through the rainforest on ziplines (see page 85).

- **Ocean Park** has excellent displays of creatures from the seas around Barbados and elsewhere, including manta rays, crabs and huge eels (see page 39).

- **Sunbury Plantation House** brings Barbados' history alive in a beautifully restored plantation house, where every room is open to the public (see page 72).

- **Holders Opera Season** and **Crop Over** are two very different festivals, the former showcasing the best of theatre, opera and classical music, and the latter a street celebration of Caribbean calypso and soca music (see pages 104–6).

Vibrant modern pottery from a craft shop in Holetown

SYMBOLS KEY
The following symbols are used throughout this book:

ⓐ address ❶ telephone ❶ fax ⓦ website address ⓔ email
🕐 opening times ❶ important

The following symbols are used on the maps:

𝒊 information office	○ city
✉ post office	○ large town
🛍 shopping	○ small town
✈ airport	■ POI (point of interest)
➕ hospital	═ motorway
🚌 bus station	━ main road
✝ cathedral	━ minor road

❶ numbers denote featured cafés, restaurants & evening venues

RESTAURANT RATINGS
The symbol after the name of each restaurant listed in this guide
indicates the price of a typical three-course meal without drinks
for one person.
£ = under BD$45   ££ = BD$45–BD$85   £££ = over BD$85

▶ *Prettily painted chattel houses*

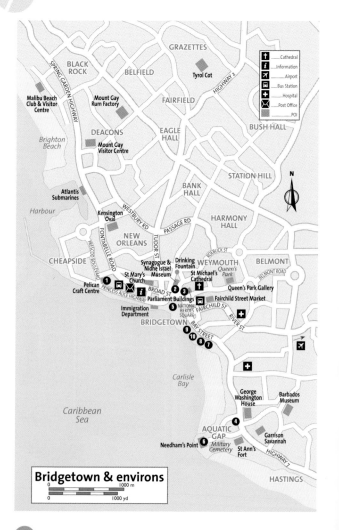

✝	Cathedral
i	Information
✈	Airport
🚌	Bus Station
✚	Hospital
✉	Post Office
■	POI

GRAZETTES

BLACK ROCK

BELFIELD

Tyrol Cot

HIGHWAY 2

Malibu Beach Club & Visitor Centre

Mount Gay Rum Factory

SPRING GARDEN HIGHWAY

FAIRFIELD

DEACONS

EAGLE HALL

BUSH HALL

Brighton Beach

Mount Gay Visitor Centre

STATION HILL

BANK HALL

N

Atlantis Submarines

WESTBURY RD

PASSAGE RD

HARMONY HALL

Harbour

Kensington Oval

NEW ORLEANS

TUDOR ST

FONTABELLE ROAD

ROEBUCK ST

WEYMOUTH

BELMONT

CHEAPSIDE

Synagogue & Nidhe Israel Museum

Drinking Fountain

Queen's Park

BELMONT ROAD

St Mary's Church

St Michael's Cathedral

Pelican Craft Centre

PRESCOD BOULEVARD

PRINCESS ALICE HIGHWAY

BROAD ST

Queen's Park Gallery

Parliament Buildings

Fairchild Street Market

Immigration Department

NATIONAL HEROES SQUARE

FAIRCHILD ST

RIVER ST

BRIDGETOWN

BAY STREET

Carlisle Bay

Caribbean Sea

✈

✚

George Washington House

Barbados Museum

AQUATIC GAP

Needham's Point

Military Cemetery

St Ann's Fort

Garrison Savannah

HIGHWAY 7

HASTINGS

Bridgetown & environs

0 ———— 1000 m
0 ———— 1000 yd

14

Bridgetown & environs

The core of Barbados' capital city is built around an inlet on the southwestern end of the island, with its main square, bus station, Parliament Buildings and the business district all within a short walk of the picturesque port area known as the Careenage. Bridgetown is the only city in Barbados and quite small, but no visit to the island would be complete without a stroll around its busy streets, where lovely colonial-era buildings compete for attention with modern office buildings, tiny shops packed with the latest fashions in clothes and shoes, and sumptuous department stores with high-quality duty-free goods. Once the jewel of Britain's Caribbean possessions, Bridgetown is now the capital of an independent nation known for its smart and stable political system, its impressive health and education records and its prosperity – and of course as one of the best places on earth for a holiday.

THINGS TO SEE & DO

Aquatic Gap & Needham's Point

Just south of Bridgetown proper is an area called Aquatic Gap where there are several restaurants and grand hotels, including the Hilton Barbados that leads to a small peninsula, Needham's Point. Nearby are an old refinery and a military cemetery dating from the colonial era. There are memorials, as well, to Barbadians who died in World Wars I and II. Needham's Point was once the site of Fort Charles, built in the 1660s and one of the earliest British colonial fortresses. It's also a good spot for swimming and snorkelling.

Barbados Museum

One of the island's most impressive attractions, Barbados Museum has exhibits on the history and culture of Barbados, local flora and fauna, natural history and documents from the island's military and slave history. There are seven galleries including one on African culture,

and another that houses exhibitions of Barbadian fine art. There is
also a library, which holds over 5,000 books, dating back to the
17th century. The building was once the British Garrison's military
prison and one of its exhibits is a cell with beds crowded into it and
iron rings on the walls.

The delightful children's museum is full of toys, clothes and
artefacts that tell the story of the country's development. There are
dressing-up opportunities and fascinating replicas of old rooms,
including one of a hut where a slave family would have lived and
a pantry of a middle-class home.

ⓐ St Ann's Garrison ⓣ 427 0201 ⓦ www.barbmuse.org.bb
ⓛ 09.00–17.00 Mon–Sat, 14.00–18.00 Sun

Bridgetown Synagogue & Nidhe Israel Museum

Some of the earliest settlers of Barbados were Jews fleeing the
Inquisition in Brazil. They began arriving in the 1650s and added their
considerable experience to the island's young sugar cane industry. The
windmills that are so much a part of the rural Barbadian landscape were
introduced by Dutch Jews, and the community grew and prospered for a
long time. With emigration, it eventually dwindled to only a few families,
but the restored synagogue and the beautifully rendered exhibits at the
Nidhe ('Scattered') Israel Museum are a fitting tribute to this community
and its history in Barbados. Also on the compound is a cemetery where a
restoration project continues and visitors can see the inscriptions on the
gravestones, some of which are in the Portuguese language of the first
Jewish immigrants.

ⓐ Synagogue Lane, near the stone drinking fountain ⓛ 08.30–16.00
Mon–Fri

Broad Street

Broad Street runs northwest from National Heroes Square and is the
centre of Bridgetown's busy business district and *the* place for duty-free
shopping. There are several gorgeous examples of colonial architecture
in Bridgetown streets and Broad Street is no exception.

⬤ *Barbados Museum, which was once the Garrison's military prison*

Carlisle Bay

Bridgetown is a capital city blessed with a most beautiful beach and body of water at Carlisle Bay. It's a popular place to relax, play sports on the sand or have a swim, and also a mooring for yachts crossing the Atlantic.

Fairchild Street Market

This fruit and vegetable market is next to the bus depot on the southern side of the Careenage (Bridgetown's estuary). It's a short stroll across the Charles Duncan O'Neal bridge from the Parliament Buildings. Saturday is the biggest market day when shoppers search out the freshest produce amid the boisterous vendors and colourful stalls.

Garrison Savannah

This peaceful, green area is a popular spot for people exercising in the early morning and evening. The island's famed racetrack is here, surrounded by colonial-era buildings, Georgian in style, including the Barbados Museum. During the 18th century, Barbados was the headquarters of the Windward and Leeward command of the British forces. At the time they were battling it out with the French for control of the region, and the Garrison is where the British regiment was stationed. Many of the Garrison buildings were handed over to Barbados in 1906 when the last British regiment left the island. There's a fine collection of cannons remaining in the Garrison area and as you walk around you get a sense of the island's proud military past. The history continues too, as the Barbados Defence Force maintains a base here at St Ann's Fort.

George Washington House

George Washington spent a few months here when he was 19, long before he began his political career. At the time Barbados was a thriving British colony, much wealthier and more sophisticated than Washington's home town in rural Virginia. The house where he and his ailing older brother, Lawrence, lived has been faithfully restored, with period furniture, both antique and replicas, recalling the style of the time. A museum upstairs gives an excellent picture of Barbadian society in the 18th and 19th centuries, including the grim reality of African slavery. There is a 15-minute film on young Washington's life in Barbados and how it is believed to have influenced his ideas and set him on the path to becoming the first President of the United States.

ⓐ Bush Hill, the Garrison ❶ 228 5461

ⓦ www.georgewashingtonbarbados.org ⓔ gwbarbados@sunbeach.net

🄻 09.00–16.30 Mon–Fri ❶ Admission charge

Kensington Oval

One of the loveliest cricket pitches in the Caribbean, Kensington Oval is the centre of the island's love affair with the game. It's thrilling just to hear the roar of the crowd on match days, but a whole lot better to actually go inside and enjoy the game – the bantering, friendly atmosphere in the stands is a big part of why cricket is so popular, and a great way to experience this important part of Barbadian culture.

ⓐ New Orleans, Bridgetown ❶ 436 1397

🔺 The gracious house George Washington lived in

Malibu Beach Club & Visitor Centre

This factory produces and exports the speciality coconut-flavoured white rum, so good with pineapple juice. The factory is on the Spring Garden Highway, near to the Mount Gay Rum Factory, and has wonderful views of the ocean. The tour shows the process of rum-making and bottling, then you can relax and enjoy a complimentary cocktail at the Malibu Beach Club.

ⓐ Spring Garden Highway ❶ 425 9393 🕒 09.00–11.00 & 12.00–16.00 Mon–Fri (tours every 30 minutes)

Mount Gay Rum Factory

Mount Gay's finishing plant gives 45-minute tours at regular intervals during the day (every hour at half past the hour). The tour begins with a video of the process of rum-making and a history of the company, which was founded in 1703. Visitors see the blending, ageing and bottling of the rum (the early stage, the actual distillation process, takes place at the company's factory in St Lucy parish in the north of the island), then are offered a complimentary cocktail. There's a shop and a bar on the premises.

ⓐ Spring Garden Highway ❶ 425 8757 Ⓦ www.mountgay.com
🕒 09.00–17.00 Mon–Fri ❶ Admission charge

National Heroes Square

This small square is situated on the northern side of the Careenage and is a focal point in the city. Although renamed in 1999 to honour ten national heroes, Bridgetown's main square still has a statue of Admiral Horatio Nelson at its centre, a matter of no small controversy on the island. The square was originally named Trafalgar Square in honour of Nelson's visit to the island in June 1805, a mere four months before he was killed at the Battle of Trafalgar, and the statue predated the British equivalent by 36 years. Among the national heroes now commemorated there are cricket legend Sir Garfield Sobers, former Prime Minister Errol Barrow and slave leader Bussa. Nearby is a memorial to Barbadians who died in the two world wars and the ornamental Fountain Gardens dating back to 1865, which were built to herald the introduction of pipe-borne water in the city.

◆ *The attractive shops at the Pelican Craft Centre*

SHOPPING

Barbados has an impressive array of high-quality imported goods, available at duty-free prices. Head to Broad Street in Bridgetown, where department stores Cave Shepherd and Harrison's, just opposite, have fine displays of tobacco, alcohol, perfume, clothes, sunglasses and gifts. For duty-free purchases, you need only show your passport and return ticket to the cashier and you can pay for your items and take them with you. Still on Broad Street, Little Switzerland is the place for watches and jewellery and there are many other stores where visitors can buy locally made craft, soaps, rum, cakes and other treats. The Pelican Craft Centre (see below) comprises about 30 shops that sell everything from locally produced skincare products to pottery, jewellery, sculpture, paintings and metalwork.

Parliament Buildings

Barbados' Parliament is one of the oldest in the world, having been established in 1639. The two legislative chambers, the House of Assembly and the Senate were moved to their current home in the 1870s. The Gothic-style buildings feature a distinctive clock tower and a courtyard framed by arches, and they form a striking landmark just off the Careenage near National Heroes Square. There is a museum in the refurbished west wing.

ⓐ Trafalgar Street Ⓦ www.barbadosparliament.com Ⓛ Open during parliamentary sessions; check dates on website

Pelican Craft Centre

This brightly hued shopping complex is just west of the Princess Alice Bus Station and features an art gallery, craft shops, as well as a variety of good-quality souvenir shops. Here you'll find some of the island's excellent pottery, basketry, wood- and metal-work, and you can peek in at workshops where artisans make various kinds of craft. There's also a cigar shop and a popular restaurant.

◯ The clock tower of the Parliament Buildings

ⓐ Princess Alice Highway ⓣ 426 0765 ⓛ 09.00–17.00 Mon–Fri, 09.00–14.00 Sat

Queen's Park Gallery

Once the residence of the British commander of the armed forces in the southern Caribbean, Queen's Park Gallery is now an art gallery featuring the works of Barbadian artists. The beautifully kept grounds surrounding the Georgian building are used as a public park and sports field.

ⓐ St Michael's Row and Crumpton Street ⓛ Art gallery: 10.00–18.00 Mon–Sat

St Mary's Church

St Mary's was built in 1827 on the site of Bridgetown's first church. A huge silk cotton tree stands on the church grounds. It was once used for public hangings and is known as the 'Justice Tree'.

ⓐ Broad Street ⓛ Often closed, but is still worth a visit

St Michael's Cathedral

The main part of St Michael's Anglican Cathedral was built in 1786 on the site of an earlier stone church dating to 1665. The island's biggest church was consecrated as a cathedral in 1825. It is open to the public during the day and visitors can take in the mahogany carvings and a beautiful relief dedicated to the island's first Bishop, William Hart Coleridge. At the eastern end, the Lady Chapel, built in 1938, has some brightly coloured stained-glass windows.

ⓐ St Michael's Row ⓛ 09.00–16.00 daily

Tyrol Cot

This exquisite residence was once home to two of Barbados' prime ministers: the island's first elected pre-Independence leader Sir Grantley Adams, after whom the airport is named, and his son Tom Adams who was prime minister from 1976 to 1985. The coral-block Caribbean/ European style home was built by William Farnum, a famed Barbadian architect of the time, in 1854, and now holds a collection of the Adamses' personal belongings. There are a series of heritage museums built on the property, including a chattel house, slave hut, rum shop and a craft centre. ⓐ Codrington Hill ⓣ 424 2074 ⓛ 08.00–16.00 Mon–Fri ⓘ Admission charge

TAKING A BREAK

Cork & Bottle £ ❶   Breezy open-air restaurant near the port, and popular with cruise ship visitors and locals alike. Good selection of Caribbean-themed dishes. ⓐ 10 Pelican Village ⓣ 426 5674 ⓔ ssrollock@yahoo.com ⓛ 11.00–16.30 Mon–Sat, closed Sun

Jenn Health & Beauty Supplies £ ❷   This health food and herbal store is a good place to stop off for a quick, healthy snack or meal: the sandwiches, vegetarian specialities and smoothies are all popular. ⓐ Corner Broad & Cowell Street ⓣ 426 1276 ⓛ 08.30–17.00 Mon–Thur, 08.30–18.00 Fri, 08.30–15.00 Sat, closed Sun

Nelson's Arms £ ❸   Busy central pub with a nautical theme to suit its name. Great place to have lunch or a snack in between shopping on Broad Street or sightseeing around the capital. ⓐ Galleria Mall, 27 Broad Street ⓣ 431 0602 ⓛ 08.00–19.00 Mon–Fri, 08.00–17.00 Sat, closed Sun

Brown Sugar ££ ❹   With a menu of excellent seafood and other Barbadian specialities and a leafy and cool atmosphere, Brown Sugar is always busy. Sunday brunch is a grand affair accompanied by steelband music. ⓐ Aquatic Gap, Bay Street ⓣ 426 7684 ⓦ www.brownsugarbarbados.com ⓔ bsugar@caribsurf.com ⓛ 12.00–14.30 & 18.00–21.30 daily

The Waterfront Café ££ ❺   Good Caribbean and international cuisine in a most delightful setting on the Careenage, across from Broad Street and the Parliament Buildings. At night there's live music to add to the friendly atmosphere. Seating at the water's edge and indoors.

🅐 Bridgetown Marina, The Careenage 🕿 427 0093
🆆 www.waterfrontcafe.com.bb 🅔 waterfrontcafe@sunbeach.net
🕒 10.00–22.00 Mon–Sat, closed Sun

The Lighthouse Terrace £££ 🅕   The Hilton's casual eatery attracts business people and families alike with its eclectic international cuisine, including the popular themed buffets and divine desserts. 🅐 Hilton

⬤ *The Careenage is a lively place to eat out*

Barbados, Needham's Point ☎ 426 0200 Ⓦ www.hiltoncaribbean.com
ⓔ bgihi_sales@hilton.com 🕑 06.30–22.30 daily

Lobster Alive £££ ❼ Serves fresh lobster on the deck of a seafood
shack, with live jazz most evenings. Added to that, Lobster Alive is set
on the idyllic Carlisle Bay, right next to the popular outdoor club,
The Boatyard. ⓐ Wesley House, Bay Street ☎ 435 0305
Ⓦ http://lobsteralive.net 🕑 12.00–15.30 & 18.00–21.00 Mon–Sat, lunch
with jazz 12.00–16.00 Sun, closed Sun eve

Wispers on the Bay £££ ❽ Wispers provides a romantic setting with
stunning views of the beach and sea and equally impressive menu of
modern Caribbean cuisine. Dining is informal but elegant and this fine
establishment is a welcome addition to the capital's culinary experience.
ⓐ Bayshore Complex, Bay Street ☎ 826 5222
Ⓦ www.wispersonthebay.com 🕑 11.30–21.30 Mon–Fri, 18.30–21.30 Sat,
closed Sun ❗ Private VIP deck

AFTER DARK

The Boatyard £££ ❾ This beach restaurant and bar is a Bridgetown
party institution, open day and night, every day of the year, with party-
goers dancing to DJ and live music until the early hours of the morning.
Cover charge for some events. ⓐ Bay Street ☎ 436 2622 Ⓦ www.
theboatyard.com ⓔ boatyard@sunbeach.net 🕑 08.00–02.00 daily

Harbour Lights £££ ❿ An open-air beachfront party venue and show
theatre, this is one of the most popular clubs in Barbados. Mondays and
Wednesdays there's dinner and a show featuring acrobats, fire-eaters,
stilt-walkers and other Crop Over festival performers. ⓐ Bay Street
☎ 436 7225 Ⓦ www.harbourlightsbarbados.com
ⓔ contactus@harbourlightsbarbados.com 🕑 19.30–03.00 Mon & Wed,
21.30–03.00 Fri, 17.00–24.00 Sun

Hastings, Rockley & Worthing

The parish of Christ Church on the south coast of Barbados is where tourism development began on the island and it continues to draw most of the holidaymakers who visit either on package tours or independently. Hastings, Rockley and Worthing are villages that follow one another eastwards along the south coast, where there is a long string of resorts, apartment hotels and guesthouses, restaurants, shops and bars. However, although the 'Strip' is packed with accommodation and entertainment, there's no great high-rise development going on and the area retains a small-island holiday charm.

The two-lane road that runs along the coast is called Highway 7 and it gets mired in traffic during rush hour, especially in the afternoon, so best to plan outings at other times. If you're travelling by minibus to go out in the evening, bear in mind that they stop running around midnight, but taxis are available after hours.

Most resorts come with a picturesque stretch of beach as well as a swimming pool, and one can easily forget about the bustle of the street if one chooses. Most people like to have both types of experiences, though, and there's always quite a lot of activity around these small towns as visitors stroll along the street from hotel to restaurant or grocery shop, taking taxis or minibuses heading west into Bridgetown or east to St Lawrence Gap or Oistins, the main town in Christ Church, in the evening. Even if you are staying on the more upmarket west coast, chances are you'll want to explore the south coast as well – it's much livelier and some of the island's finest restaurants and most popular hang-outs can be found here, as well as lovely beaches.

BEACHES

South coast beaches are favoured by windsurfers and bodysurfers as the breezes whip up the waves to medium height in this area. All beaches in Barbados are public and the government rules that there must be public access to beaches, even those that are faced by exclusive resorts.

⬥ *The beach by Coconut Court Beach Hotel*

Rockley Beach

Locals call this beach Accra because of the so-named resort that dominates this corner of Rockley. It is a magnificent, long arc of white sand that's one of the liveliest on the island. It's popular with both locals and visitors and at any time in the day you can have a swim or a walk, go waterskiing, bodysurfing or have your hair braided, join those relaxing or working on their tans – and with all the activity it's also a prime spot for people-watching. There's an area off the beach with craft and souvenir booths – which means there are only a few people selling bead necklaces and other keepsakes on the beach itself, so you can generally relax in peace – as well as a couple of places to go for a drink and a snack if you're not in a hurry to get back to the hotel.

Sandy Beach, Pink Pearl Beach, Casuarina Beach are all east of Rockley and are also beautiful beaches within the south coast tourist area popular with windsurfers or for anyone seeking some fun and sun on the beach.

Worthing Beach

Just east of Rockley is the beautiful white sand beach of Worthing. The sea in this area offers a variety of delights, with a coral reef teeming with tropical fish just offshore. On the inside of the reef the calm and relatively shallow waters make it a good place for children to swim. The western part of the beach is deeper with more lively waves, suitable for stronger swimmers and those who enjoy watersports.

THINGS TO SEE & DO

Rockley Golf & Country Club

Part of the all-inclusive Club Rockley residential development, the course has a simple 9-hole 18-tee layout, with another nine holes playable from various tee positions. This is the oldest golf course in Barbados and its Tee Off Bar and Restaurant is said to be the most friendly club bar on the island.

ⓐ Rockley ☏ 435 7873 ⓦ http://rockleygolfclub.com
ⓔ teetime@rockleygolfclub.com

Stargaze at the Harry Bayley Observatory

The Barbados Astronomical Society has its headquarters here and the public is allowed in on Friday evenings to look at the stars, weather permitting. Built in 1963, this observatory is still one of the most advanced in the Caribbean.

ⓐ Clapham, south of Highway 6 ⓣ 426 1317 ⓛ 21.00 Fri, if the weather is good; best to call ahead ⓘ Admission fee

Watersports

The south coast offers watersports fun for everyone: calm swimming, snorkelling over inshore reefs and tidal pools, jet skiing, and its waters make perfect conditions for windsurfing.

Charles Watersports ⓐ Dover Beach, Christ Church ⓣ 428 9550

TAKING A BREAK

Bert's £ Great atmosphere and full of personality, just like the proprietor, Bert Inniss. The other owner, Eugene Melnyk, also owns the Ottawa Senators hockey team, and if you share Canadians' passion for ice hockey you'll love game nights on multiple flat-screen TVs. The pub food and cocktails are excellent, too. ⓐ Rockley ⓣ 435 7924 ⓦ www.bertsbarbados.com ⓔ info@bertsbarbados.com ⓛ 11.30–22.30 daily

Carib Beach Bar £ Barbados-shaped bar caters to a good mix of families and singles, locals and visitors, and has a great view of Sandy Beach and its gentle lagoon. The menu features seafood, sandwiches and hearty salads. ⓐ The Stream, Second Avenue, Hastings ⓣ 435 8540 ⓔ caribbeachbar@sunbeach.net ⓛ 11.00–22.00 daily ⓘ Bare feet are acceptable but not bare backs: a shirt is required for dinner.

Guang Dong Chinese Restaurant & Bar £ The most popular Chinese restaurant on the island, Guang Dong is known for dependable, basic Chinese food in a no-frills setting. ⓐ The Stream, Third Avenue, Worthing ⓣ 435 7387 ⓛ 11.00–23.00 daily

Just Grillin' **£** This open-air eatery on the boardwalk of Quayside Centre, a small shopping plaza, is popular for lunch or dinner, or just for hanging out and having a few margaritas and snacks. Many visitors staying in the area (it is directly opposite the Accra Beach Resort) find themselves here more than once during their stay because of its freshly grilled seafood and meats, convenient location and laid-back atmosphere. ⓐ Quayside Centre, Highway 7, Rockley ❶ 435 6469 ⓦ www.justgrillinbarbados.com ❶ 11.30–22.00 Mon–Sat, 17.30–22.00 Sun

Apsara/Tamnak Thai £ These are two distinct restaurants, one Indian, the other Thai, housed in different parts of a renovated 200-year-old house, with sumptuous décor to match the exotic cuisine. ⓐ Morecambe House, Worthing ❶ 435 5454 ⓦ www.apsarabarbados.com ⓔ info@apsarabarbados.com ❶ 11.30–22.00 Mon–Fri, 18.00–22.00 Sat & Sun ❶ Private room available

Bistro Monet £ Large portions of tasty Caribbean and international food, reasonable prices and a relaxed atmosphere all make this a very popular restaurant, even though it may not have the most scenic of views. ⓐ Healthy Horizons Building, Hastings Main Road ❶ 435 9389 ❶ 11.00–22.00 Mon–Fri, 18.00–22.00 Sat, closed Sun

Bubba's Sports Bar £ There are two levels of entertainment at this American-style sports bar – no smoking on the upper level. Several television screens give sports fans a chance to watch their favourite games while partaking of drinks and a good menu of pub fare, including burgers, fries and wings. ⓐ Rockley Main Road ❶ 435 6217 ⓦ www.bubbassportsbar.net ⓔ bubbas2@caribsurf.com ❶ 11.30–23.00 Mon–Thur, 11.30–01.00 Fri–Sat, 08.00–23.00 Sun ❶ Opening hours vary to suit timing of sports events

Il Forno £ Authentic Italian cuisine at two locations: at the water's edge in Hastings and at the Sheraton Mall (north of St Lawrence Gap). There's always pizza – theirs is cooked in a special wood-fired brick oven – as a good choice for a lighter meal or when you have ravenous young people to feed. ⓐ Caribee Hotel, Hastings and Sheraton Mall ⓣ 426 1956 ⓦ www.ilforno barbados.com ⓛ 11.30–22.00 Mon–Thur, 11.30–23.00 Fri & Sat, closed Sun

Mama Mia Italian Deli and Pizzeria ££ A cosy and casual spot right on the main road near the Garrison historic area. Mama Mia is famous for its classic Italian dishes, pizza made in a traditional wood-burning oven, lighter fare like salads and panini, and rich desserts. ⓐ Hastings Main Road ⓣ 434 3354 ⓦ www.mamamiadeli.com ⓛ 08.30–21.00 Mon–Sat, closed Sun

Opa! Greek Restaurant ££ Opa! features a Greek-inspired menu and is known for its warm atmosphere and great staff. The trendy décor and perfect spot on the beach at Rockley also add to its appeal. ⓐ Shak Shak Complex, Hastings Main Road ⓣ 435 1234 ⓛ 10.00–22.00 Mon–Fri, 18.00–22.00 Sat & Sun

Patisserie and Bistro Flindt ££ Fresh sandwiches, salads and out-of-this-world desserts are the signature pieces at this busy but quiet spot for lunch and breakfast. They make their own breads and desserts and also offer a take-out menu. ⓐ Rockley ⓣ 435 2600 ⓦ www.flindtbarbados.com ⓔ flindt@flindtbarbados.com ⓛ 07.00–18.00 Mon–Fri, 07.30–14.00 Sat, 07.30–12.00 Sun

Thirty-Nine Steps Bistro ££ This homey restaurant in a busy shopping plaza has stood the test of time with its reasonably priced, tasty, eclectic food, live entertainment and dancing on some nights. ⓐ Chattel Plaza, Hastings ⓣ 427 0715 ⓛ 12.00–21.30 daily

Aqua Restaurant & Lounge £££ This is a chic beachfront restaurant, known for its excellent Caribbean and international cuisine. There are theme nights (Wednesday is Japanese, Lobster Fest on Saturday) and a

formal afternoon tea. ⓐ Keswick Court, Hastings ⓣ 420 2995
ⓦ www.aquabarbados.com ⓔ info@aquabarbados.com ⓛ 12.00–22.00
Mon–Fri, 18.30–22.00 Sat & Sun

Champers Wine Bar & Restaurant £££ This is simply one of the best
dining experiences on the island, with excellent Caribbean cuisine with
an emphasis on fresh seafood, great but unobtrusive service and the
most pleasant, romantic setting overlooking the ocean and Rockley
Beach. With all this, Champers also has a warm and relaxed atmosphere
and is usually packed with business people and tourists at lunchtime.

⬤ *The beautiful view from Champers Wine Bar and Restaurant*

ⓐ Skeete's Hill, Rockley ⓣ 434 3463 ⓦ www.champersbarbados.com
ⓔ champersinc@caribsurf.com ⓛ 11.30–22.00 Mon–Sat, 18.00–22.00 Sun

AFTER DARK

Restaurants

Lucky Horseshoe Saloon & Steakhouse £ This loud and friendly venue is popular with families, singles and sports fans alike, and is also a good bet when hunger strikes after a night of partying. The Wild West-style 'saloon' serves steaks, burgers and other favourites of the comfort-food variety, and there's non-stop fun if you wish, with several television screens showing sports and slot machines to keep you busy. There's also a deck for those who want a bit of quiet.
ⓐ Worthing Main Road ⓣ 425 5825 ⓦ www.luckyh.com
ⓛ 24 hours daily

Shakers Bar & Grill £ This small eatery set in a chattel house is a bit off the beaten track, but is nevertheless a favourite. The owners are as much appreciated by their regular clientele as the great food they serve.
ⓐ Browne's Gap, Rockley ⓣ 228 8855 ⓛ 18.00–22.00 Tues–Sun, closed Mon ⓘ Credit cards not accepted

Wytukai Restaurant ££ The only Polynesian restaurant on the island, Wytukai is treasured for its exotic cuisine as well as its chic décor and setting in one of the south coast's best-known resorts. ⓐ Accra Beach Hotel & Resort, Rockley ⓣ 435 8920 ⓦ www.accrabeachhotel.com
ⓛ 18.30–22.30 Tues–Sat, closed Sun & Mon

Nightlife

Club Xtreme £££ With three 'zones' of partying – a main party area, a more laid-back lounge and a games room – this club is often packed with young people dancing to the latest in Caribbean and international sounds. ⓐ Worthing Main Road ⓣ 435 4455 ⓦ www.clubxtreme.net
ⓔ info@cafesolbarbados.com ⓛ 22.00–04.00 Tues & Sat

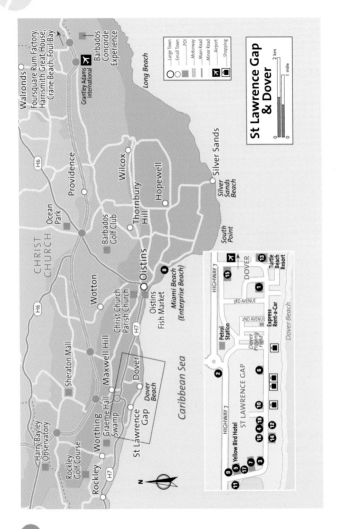

St Lawrence Gap & Dover

St Lawrence Gap & Dover

East along the south coast from Worthing on Highway 7 is the trendiest street in Barbados: the famed St Lawrence Gap – though just saying 'The Gap' will do. This is where all the action is on the south coast in the evenings, where tourists and, to a lesser extent, locals flock to fine restaurants, watch their favourite sports at hyperactive sports bars, go club-hopping and dance to the latest reggae, soca (dance music that originated in Trinidad), hip hop or golden oldies until the early hours of the next morning. There's often a mix of age groups and in one venue you may find some people dining or having drinks, while in another corner local youngsters contort themselves to perform the latest Jamaican dancehall moves, while on the street side others sit back and watch the hip human traffic go by.

There's not much happening during the day, but the beaches here are lovely and perfect for recovering from a strenuous night out. Other daytime activities include watersports, beach cricket or football and the Sheraton Mall is just north of this area if shopping is on the agenda. There are also some attractions within a short minibus or taxi ride and still within the parish of Christ Church.

BEACHES

Dover Beach is smack in the middle of the St Lawrence Gap area. It's one of the best-loved beaches in the south of Barbados, with waters calm and clear enough for swimming and snorkelling but also with plenty of action for watersports enthusiasts, with sailing, jet-skiing, boogie boarding and windsurfing. There are refreshment booths and shops nearby, and, depending on the season, you can see cricket or football being played at the Dover playing field across the road.

Silver Sands, with its glistening, energetic waters, is a windsurfing paradise that attracts fans of the sport from all over the world. The village has a cool tropical vibe and so even people who aren't willing to go into the often-rough water or who aren't surfers find it a pleasant place to spend a few hours.

● The Concorde Experience is a great day out

Long Beach is the longest beach on the island. It's a beautiful, picturesque beach that is often deserted because the water can be choppy. It's also a great choice for long walks among the driftwood-strewn sands, but as a safety precaution make sure you go with company.

THINGS TO SEE & DO

Barbados Concorde Experience
You can get a taste of what it was like to fly on the fastest passenger aircraft ever built here on the ground in Barbados. The Concorde Experience features an interactive flight school, departure lounge, observation deck and an in-flight multi-media presentation. It's one of Barbados' most exciting attractions – fun, educational and fascinating. ⓐ Grantley Adams International Airport, Seawell ❶ 253 6257 ⓦ www.barbadosconcorde.com ⓔ info@barbadosconcorde.com ❶ 09.00–18.00 daily ❶ Admission charge

Ocean Park
A big hit with children and adults alike, Ocean Park is a beautifully landscaped aquarium with imaginative displays of all types of marine life. There are moray eels, crabs, piranhas, sharks, sea horses and tropical reef fish, plus the chance to feed the stingrays. Afterwards, head to the adjacent water park for some noisy fun. There's also a mini-golf course, a shop and a snackbar at Ocean Park, making it good for at least a couple hours of education and fun. ⓐ Balls Complex ❶ 420 7405 ⓦ www.oceanparkbarbados.com ❶ 09.00–19.00 daily ❶ Admission charge; additional cost for mini-golf

TAKING A BREAK

Bean and Bagel £ ❶ Sandwiches, light meals and salads are the specialities here, and together with great coffee and an internet café, they make it one of the popular hang-outs at the eastern end of the Gap. ⓐ St Lawrence Gap ❶ 420 4604 ❶ 07.00–15.30 daily

New Century Chinese Restaurant £ ❷ A second storey has been added to this restaurant at the top of the St Lawrence Road. It's a sound choice for inexpensive Chinese food, served promptly and in good-sized portions. An English menu is available as well, and they offer takeaway and also deliver to places nearby. ⓐ St Lawrence Main Road (Highway 7) ❶ 420 2822 ⏱ 11.00–23.00 daily

Café Sol ££ ❸ Hearty, reasonably priced Mexican dishes and generous margaritas are the trademarks of this warm and cosy restaurant and bar. ⓐ St Lawrence Gap ❶ 420 7655 ⓦ www.cafesolbarbados.com ⓔ info@cafesolbarbados.com ⏱ 12.00–23.00 daily

Captain's Carvery/The Deck ££ ❹ The Carvery's table, filled with various meats and side orders, is the hot speciality for dinner guests, but this huge pub with its popular Bajan buffet is also a good choice for lunch. ⓐ The Ship Inn, St Lawrence Gap ❶ 435 6961 ⓦ www.shipinnbarbados.com ⓔ info@shipinnbarbados.com ⏱ 12.00–22.30 daily

Flying Fish ££ ❺ The restaurant is located on the ground floor of a hotel looking out to the picturesque Little Bay. It's known for its warm, friendly atmosphere and Bajan and British fare, including formal afternoon tea. ⓐ Yellow Bird Hotel, St Lawrence Gap ❶ 418 9772 ⓦ www.yellowbirdbarbados.com ⓔ info@yellowbirdbarbados.com ⏱ 07.00–22.00 daily

Steak House and Seafood Grill ££ ❻ Succulent steaks, hefty burgers, and other robust fare have been the trademark of this popular grill for 20 years; there's also seafood for those who want something lighter. ⓐ St Lawrence Gap ❶ 428 7152 ⏱ 13.00–22.00 daily

Sweet Potatoes ££ ❼ Tasty Barbadian cuisine, served in generous portions. The style is quite laid-back and casual, so plan to 'lime' (hang out) a while. ⓐ St Lawrence Gap ❶ 435 9638 ⏱ 11.30–22.15 daily

🔺 *Enthralled by a ray at Ocean Park*

Café Luna £££ ❽ This rooftop restaurant overlooks the perfect Enterprise Beach in one of Barbados' most charming boutique hotels. The eclectic Mediterranean menu is very fresh and creative, and there's always something new. Great sushi specials on Thursday and Friday nights. ❸ Little Arches Hotel, Enterprise Coast Road ❶ 420 4689 Ⓦ www.littlearches.com Ⓔ paradise@littlearches.com ⏱ 08.00–21.30 daily

Coast Restaurant & Bar £££ ❾ This recent addition to the Gap experience serves New World cuisine with imaginative European and Bajan hints. ❸ 1 St Lawrence Gap ❶ 418 9992 Ⓦ www.coastbarbados.com Ⓔ coastbarbados@gmail.com ⏱ 12.00–22.30 Tues–Sat, 18.00–22.30 Sun, closed Mon

● *Long Beach is a beautiful and quiet spot*

AFTER DARK

Restaurants

Aquapisce ££  **❿** Known for its friendly, family-style service and excellent Bajan fish and seafood dishes, Aquapisce also has a children's menu and an extensive wine list. Also serves beef, lamb and pork dishes.
🄰 St Lawrence Gap 🅣 420 8353 🄻 18.00–21.45 Mon–Sat, closed Sun

Bellini's Trattoria ££ **⓫** This restaurant has a great Italian menu served in a romantic ambience, overlooking the ocean but still in the thick of things at St Lawrence Gap. 🄰 Little Bay Hotel 🅣 420 7587
🅦 www.littlebayhotelbarbados.com 🄴 little_bay@caribsurf.com
🄻 18.00–22.30 daily

Harlequin ££  ⑫　Harlequin's bright, lively décor, superb service and excellent, eclectic cuisine are enough to justify its good reputation. Add its children's menu and the way the staff caters to the whole family and you have a sure winner. ⓐ St Lawrence Gap ⓣ 420 7677 ⓦ www.harlequinrestaurant.com ⓔ harlequin@sunbeach.net ⓛ 18.00–21.30 daily

Asiagos £££ ⑬　Asiagos serves authentic Italian cuisine in an elegant trattoria overlooking beautiful Turtle Bay. The bustle and the audacity of their open kitchen is a hit with diners. ⓐ Turtle Beach Resort, Dover ⓣ 428 7131 ⓦ www.turtlebeachresortbarbados.com ⓛ 19.00–21.00 Tues–Sun, closed Mon ⓘ Elegant dress code, and only children 12 years and older allowed

🔺 *Silver Sands is a windsurfer's dream*

Josef's £££ ⑭ Away from the activity of the Gap strip, this elegant and romantic restaurant's cliff-side setting and gourmet Caribbean-Asian fusion cuisine make it one of the best-loved on the island. Upstairs is Kampai Restaurant, for delectable contemporary Japanese cuisine. ⓐ St Lawrence Gap ⓣ 420 7638 ⓦ www.josefsinbarbados.com ⓔ josefsrestaurant@hotmail.com ⓛ 18.30–22.00 daily

Luigi's Ristorante Italiano £££ ⑮ Luigi's is a warm, welcoming family restaurant. It features an extensive menu of Italian favourites, home-made pasta, cheeses from their own cheese factory on the island and wines imported from Italy. ⓐ Dover Woods ⓣ 428 9218 ⓦ www.luigisbarbados.com ⓔ dine@luigisbarbados.com ⓛ 18.30–21.45 Mon–Sat, closed Sun

Nightlife

Club NXS ££ ⑯ This new club offers many ways to pass the evening, from just 'liming' at the bar or dancing to live music, to relaxing in the private VIP areas. ⓐ St Lawrence Gap ⓣ 262 4000 ⓛ 16.00–04.00 daily ⓘ Admission charge for some shows and parties; no cover charge for bar

Jumbie's ££ ⑰ This popular bar and restaurant feels like a party all the time, with DJ and live music some nights, so people can start with a meal and drinks on the outdoor patio facing St Lawrence Bay and the busy street – good for people-watching – and graduate to the dance area to work off some calories. ⓐ St Lawrence Gap ⓣ 420 7615 ⓛ 16.00–03.00 daily

The Ship Inn ££ ⑱ Always a hotspot, the sprawling restaurant, sports bar and dance club features live local soca stars and other musicians, and is one of the must-dos of Bajan nightlife. ⓐ St Lawrence Gap ⓣ 420 7447 ⓦ www.shipinnbarbados.com ⓔ info@shipinnbarbados.com ⓛ 12.00–03.00 daily

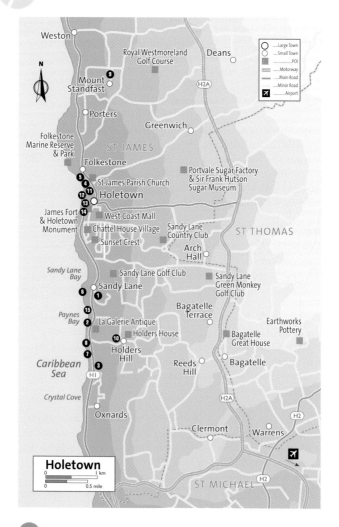

Holetown

Holetown is north of Bridgetown along Highway 1. This is where English sailors first set foot on the island in 1625. Holetown was once the heavily fortified centre of British presence on the island, but its importance dimmed when the present capital, Bridgetown, was built in an area with natural harbours that made it easier to defend. Modern Holetown is once again an important hub as it benefits from the huge amount of upmarket tourism development on this so-called 'Platinum Coast'.

Many visitors to its fabulously expensive hotels tend to stay within the privacy of their resorts, but there is much to enjoy in the area. The town retains several reminders of its colonial heritage, but there's nothing old-fashioned about this trendy little town of shops, restaurants, craft stores, exclusive resorts and a beautiful bay.

BEACHES

The west coast, lying on the Caribbean Sea, has many of the most idyllic beaches in Barbados. In this area, they are narrower than those further south and north but the sand is fine and white, the water calm and turquoise, and the sunsets over the perfect sea are brilliant and mesmerising.

Paynes Bay, south of Holetown, is one of the most popular beaches on the west coast and a favourite with families at the weekend. There's good swimming and snorkelling as well as watersports, especially jet-skiing and sailing. There are lots of exclusive hotels, villas, restaurants and bars in the area. It's usually quite relaxed here but gets busier when cruise ship visitors arrive from Bridgetown Harbour to enjoy a day at the seaside.

Just north of Paynes Bay and a little south of Holetown is **Sandy Lane Bay**, home of the deluxe Sandy Lane Hotel, famed in the Caribbean for its elegance and its celebrity guests. Public access is at the southern perimeter of the hotel and it's well worth a visit, for a jet-ski ride, a swim or even just a stroll along the length of its splendid mahogany tree-lined beach.

RESORTS

THINGS TO SEE & DO

Bagatelle Great House

Like Holders House (see below) this is a wonderful example of the great Barbadian plantation house. It got its name after its owner gambled it away in a game of dice in 1877 and thereafter, to save face, referred to it as a 'mere bagatelle'. Now the setting of an elegant restaurant and tearoom, the rest of the building is open to visitors during restaurant opening hours.

ⓐ Bagatelle, St Thomas ⓣ 421 6767 ⓛ 12.00–18.00 Mon & Tues, 12.00–14.30 Wed–Fri, 12.00–22.00 Sat, closed Sun

Folkestone Marine Reserve & Park

Good opportunity to swim with the fish and sometimes marine turtles in this closed-off reserve area, or snorkel along a coral reef. It's a popular picnic spot for families. Lockers, fins and snorkelling gear can be rented.

ⓐ Folkestone, St James ⓣ 422 2314 ⓛ 09.00–17.00 Mon–Fri, closed Sat & Sun

Golf

Royal Westmoreland Golf Course This stunning and challenging Robert Trent Jones II-designed 18-hole championship golf course has spectacular views of the sea. ⓐ St James ⓣ 422 4653 ⓦ www.royalwestmoreland.com ⓔ villarental@royal-westmoreland.com

Sandy Lane Golf Club This fabulous five-star resort has three breathtaking golf courses: the Sandy Lane Old Nine; the 18-hole Country Club and the 18-hole Green Monkey, which has been named as one of the Caribbean's best by golf aficionados. ⓐ Sandy Lane, St James ⓣ 444 2000 ⓦ www.sandylane.com

Holders House

This sprawling estate, complete with a grand plantation house and a polo field, is the venue for one of the Caribbean's premier performing

Sandy Lane is one of the top golf resorts in the world

arts festivals. Holders Opera Season is held in March, with the dome of the sky and gigantic samaan trees serving as concert hall for a host of top international and Caribbean stars. The private home is closed to the public for much of the year, but polo matches are held on scheduled Saturday afternoons.

ⓐ Holders Hill, St James ⓦ www.holders.net ⓔ theseason@holders.net
ⓣ Arts Festival: 432 6385; Barbados Polo Club: 432 1802

SHOPPING

Being a trendy and upmarket town, Holetown's souvenir shops are naturally a tad more tasteful than in some other places, and there are quite a lot of duty-free shops to keep you away from the beach for a while. Most of the stores are on or near the main road, Highway 1, and there are shopping centres (**Sunset Crest** and the **West Coast Mall**) where you can get just about anything you need.

Chattel House Village (ⓐ Highway 1, south Holetown ⓛ 09.00–17.00 Mon–Sat, 09.00–13.00 Sun) is a series of prettily painted shops in the style of traditional Barbadian chattel houses, set in a landscaped plaza. The original chattel houses were simple wooden houses built by the early African plantation workers. They could easily be dismantled and moved from one plantation to another. The **Best of Barbados** shop is here, with local artwork, aromatic beauty products, candles and island souvenirs on offer, as well as an art gallery, gourmet food shop, beachwear and T-shirt shops. Take a drive to **Earthworks Pottery** (ⓐ 2 Edghill Heights, St Thomas ⓣ 425 0223 ⓦ www.earthworks-pottery.com ⓛ 09.00–17.00 Mon–Fri, 09.00–13.00 Sat, closed Sun), famous for its blue-and-green pottery; or just south to Paynes Bay where **La Galerie Antique** is packed with wonderful silverware, china and furniture that once graced the homes of the plantocracy. It's a fascinating shop, more like a museum dedicated to the colonial era.

⬥ *Holders House has a tropical charm*

James Fort & Holetown Monument

At the centre of Holetown, a few iron cannons mark the spot where James Fort once stood, and is now the site of a police station. Near to the cannons is the Holetown Monument, built in 1905 to commemorate the arrival of the first British settlers in February 1627.

St James Parish Church

The oldest and one of the most beautiful Anglican churches on the island. The original wooden building was constructed in 1628, but replaced with a stone structure in 1660. There were more alterations between 1789 and 1874 after hurricanes and fires destroyed parts of the building, but there remain some relics from the 1600s.

ⓐ Folkestone ❶ 422 4117 🕐 09.00–17.00 daily

Sugar factory & museum

Portvale Sugar Factory is a working sugar factory that visitors can tour during the reaping season in the first six months of the year. Next door, the **Sir Frank Hutson Sugar Museum** welcomes visitors all year round to its comprehensive exhibition on the history and production of sugar in Barbados, which was the mainstay of the island's economy before tourism took over.

ⓐ West of Highway 2A ❶ 426 2421 🕐 08.00–17.00 Mon–Sat, closed Sun
❶ Admission charge

TAKING A BREAK

The Beach House ££ ❶   Caribbean–Mediterranean cuisine is served in a canopied beachfront setting that makes the most of the fabulous west coast sunsets. Their Bajan buffets are very popular. Live jazz on Fridays.
ⓐ Sandy Lane ❶ 432 1163 🕸 www.thebeachhousebarbados.com
🕐 11.00–23.00 Mon–Sat, 11.00–18.00 Sun

Blue Monkey Bar & Restaurant ££ ❷   Casual eatery that serves local specialities, some with an interesting twist, like their superb lobster burger. It's conveniently situated right on the beach and is very popular, especially with tourists. ⓐ Paynes Bay ⓣ 432 7528 ⓛ 11.00–23.00 daily

Cariba Restaurant & Bar ££ ❸   A relatively new addition to the west coast scene, Cariba is set in a delightfully decorated chattel house a bit off the main highway. The Bajan cuisine is top-notch and its local owners warm and friendly – the chef makes it a point to come out and chat with diners. ⓐ 1 Clarke's Gap, Derricks, St James ⓣ 432 8737 ⓛ 18.00–21.30 Tues–Sat, 12.00–21.30 Sun, closed Mon

Sitar Indian Restaurant ££ ❹   Authentic Indian cuisine isn't easy to come by on the west coast and Sitar provides a haven for those who crave mouth-watering curries and smouldering tandooris. ⓐ Second Street, Holetown ⓣ 432 2248 ⓛ 18.00–22.30 daily

Spago ££ ❺   Spago has two branches in Holetown, which serve superb pizzas and Italian dinners. The newer of the two, at Settlers Beach, has a lovely sea view. ⓐ Second Street & Settlers Beach Hotel, Holetown ⓣ 432 7394 & 422 3052 ⓦ www.spagobarbados.com ⓛ 11.30–23.00 (Second Street) 08.00–23.00 (Settlers Beach) daily

Bajan Blue £££ ❻   Beach-front restaurant at the exclusive and luxurious Sandy Lane Resort. Menu is Caribbean–Mediterranean; there are theme nights and its exquisite Sunday lunch buffets are legendary. ⓐ Sandy Lane Resort ⓣ 444 2000 ⓦ www.sandylane.com ⓛ 07.00–22.00 daily

The Cliff £££ ❼   A hugely romantic cliff-top restaurant that's been a favourite with discerning gourmands for many years, The Cliff features fine international cuisine with a definite Asian leaning. ⓐ Derricks, St James ⓣ 432 1922 ⓦ www.thecliffbarbados.com ⓔ thecliff@sunbeach.net ⓛ 18.30–22.00 daily (Dec–Apr); 18.30–22.00 Mon–Sat, closed Sun (May–Nov)

Daphne's £££ ❽ Italian–Caribbean fusion is the cuisine at this sophisticated restaurant that's beside the beach at a lovely bay. The menu features interesting use of ingredients and some excellent vegetarian dishes; it's great for a special evening. ⓐ House Hotel, Paynes Bay ❶ 432 2731 ⓦ www.daphnesbarbados.com ❶ 12.30–15.00 & 18.30–21.30 daily

Sassafras £££ ❾ This restaurant has moved from its former location at Derricks to a residential resort, but its impeccably prepared Asian fusion cuisine, surprisingly reasonable prices and its laid-back style have not

▲ *The Cliff is exclusive but wonderful*

changed – in fact Sassafras is better than ever. ⓐ Sugar Hill Resort, Mt Standfast, St James ⓣ 422 6644 ⓦ www.sassafras246.com ⓔ sassafras@sunbeach.net ⓛ 12.00–17.00 Tues, Thur & Sat, 12.00–22.00 Wed & Fri, 11.30–17.00 Sun, closed Mon

AFTER DARK

Marshall's ££ ⑩ This laid-back bar opposite the Holders polo field serves trusty Bajan fare: flying fish, stewed meats plus macaroni pie and

◆ *The west coast beaches are calm and idyllic*

other tasty staples. It's also something of a cricket-lovers' den, with cricketing mementos everywhere and often a few of the sport's heroes dropping in. ⓐ Holders Hill ⓑ 12.00–14.00 & 17.00–21.00 daily

Lexy Piano Bar £££ ⑪   Always lively, Lexy is a great hang-out for anyone who enjoys a good sing-along in great company. ⓐ Second Street, Holetown ⓣ 432 5399 ⓦ www.lexypianobar.com
ⓔ info@lexypianobar.com ⓑ 18.00–03.00 daily in season (Nov–Mar)

The Mews £££ ⑫   A Holetown institution, The Mews serves sumptuous eclectic cuisine in a romantic colonial-style home. At night the scene changes to a lively bar. Live music on Fridays. ⓐ Second Street, Holetown ⓣ 432 1122 ⓑ 18.30–24.00 Mon–Sat, closed Sun

Olive's Bar and Bistro £££ ⑬   This chic cocktail bar and restaurant is housed in a coral-stone colonial-style building, full of character and breezy atmosphere. It's a cool place to hang out, with live entertainment in the high season months between December and March. ⓐ Second Street, Holetown ⓣ 432 2112 ⓑ 18.30–22.00 daily

Ragamuffins Bar & Restaurant £££ ⑭   Chattel house venue with a congenial, fun atmosphere and terrific Bajan cuisine – the blackened fish with garlic aoli is the signature dish. Don't miss the hoot of a drag show on Sundays, but book in advance. ⓐ First Street, Holetown ⓣ 432 1295 ⓦ www.ragamuffinsbarbados.com ⓔ raga@caribsurf.com ⓑ 17.30–24.00 Sun–Fri, closed Sat

Scarlet £££ ⑮   The cool décor with 60s Pop Art prints belies the warm, folksy atmosphere of this most pleasant bar. Scarlet serves great cocktails and local food as well. ⓐ Paynes Bay, St James ⓣ 432 3663 ⓑ 17.00–24.00 daily

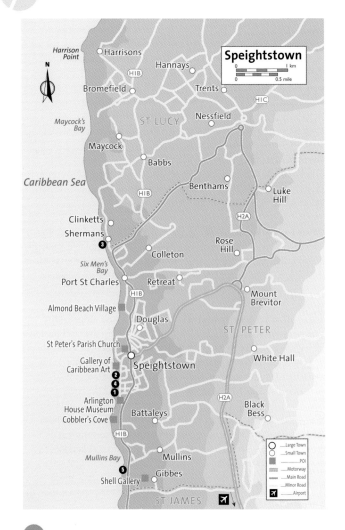

Speightstown

Speightstown

Speightstown (pronounced 'Spitestown') is the second largest town in Barbados and was once a bustling port city and commercial centre. Its star has faded somewhat over the centuries and it has not reaped the great rewards from the robust tourist development further south. However, there are some beautiful colonial-era Georgian buildings that are still standing on its main strip, Queen Street, and there is continuing restoration work to reclaim some of its past glory and make it into a model town, architecturally.

St Peter's Parish Church is located here, with its airy and pleasant interior, restored stone walls and clock tower. Speightstown has an air of quiet elegance about it, with wide main streets and a relaxed atmosphere, and a walk around the business area gives a hint of how it must have been in its heyday. More colonial-type buildings can be found in the narrow streets off the main shopping area. **Almond Beach Village** and **Cobbler's Cove** are two resorts nearby, both with gorgeous beaches, and there are several top-class restaurants and lively pubs in the town.

BEACHES

South of Speightstown is **Mullins Bay**, a short stretch of pristine beach just off the main road and a favourite stop-off point for bus tours. There's a popular restaurant and beach bar and people are often stretched out on deckchairs under umbrellas lazily enjoying the scene, swimmers paddling in the water and jet-skiers whizzing by. North of Speightstown is **Port St Charles**, a luxury residential development and marina. Just beyond that is the village on **Six Men's Bay**, a lovely beach with colourful fishing boats on the sand, a picturesque Bajan scene quite different from the ostentatious wealth of Port St Charles. **Maycock's Bay** near the tip of the west coast and just south of Harrison Point and its lighthouse, is the site of the ruins of Maycock's Fort, a 17th-century stalwart of defence for the island. The bay itself is lovely and a good spot to stretch your legs.

◐ *A hotel pool by the sea at Cobbler's Cove*

THINGS TO SEE & DO

Arlington House Museum

This new museum features a high-tech, interactive experience of Barbadian history in a beautifully restored colonial home.

ⓐ Queen Street ⓣ 422 4064 ⓛ 09.00–17.00 Mon–Sat, closed Sun
ⓘ Admission charge

Gallery of Caribbean Art

The gallery showcases the work of the finest painters, sculptors and photographers in Barbados and the Caribbean region.

ⓐ Northern Business Centre, Queen Street ⓣ 419 0858 ⓛ 09.30–16.30 Mon–Fri, 09.30–14.00 Sat, closed Sun

St Peter's Parish Church

This church is one of the oldest in Barbados, originally built around 1630 and rebuilt after it was destroyed by a hurricane in 1831. St Peter's was again destroyed in 1980, this time by fire, but has been restored to its present, quiet beauty.

ⓐ Church Street ⓛ 09.00–17.00 daily

Shell Gallery

Hundreds of shells of all types can be seen and bought at this shop. They are available both individually and as part of art creations, jewellery, mirrors and picture frames.

ⓐ Gibbes, St Peter ⓣ 422 2593 ⓛ 09.00–17.00 Mon–Fri, 09.00–14.00 Sat, closed Sun

TAKING A BREAK

Back to Eden £ ⓘ This busy vegetarian restaurant in a shopping plaza features tasty local dishes, healthy specialities and a large selection of juices from in-season fruit. ⓐ Jordan's Plaza, Queen Street, Speightstown
ⓣ 422 0410 ⓛ 10.00–16.00 Mon–Fri, closed Sat & Sun

Fisherman's Pub £££ ❷   This seaside restaurant and bar started off as a typical Bajan 'rum shop', but over the years it has become quite a gathering place for tourists, while still retaining its local flavour. Drinks, the Creole buffet and a ringside view of the dramatic western sunset are all part of its appeal, plus there are dance parties on some nights. ⓐ Queen Street, Speightstown ❶ 422 2703 ❷ 11.00–13.00 Mon, Tues, Thur & Sat, 11.00–03.00 Wed & Fri, 12.00–24.00 Sun

The Fish Pot £££ ❸   The chef at this eclectic seafood restaurant has come up with a fresh approach and a wide variety of dishes, from panini and salads to pastas, curries and divine desserts. The Fish Pot is part of a resort community of luxury guest cottages. ⓐ Little Good Harbour, Shermans ❶ 439 3000 Ⓦ www.littlegoodharbourbarbados.com ❷ 08.30–22.00 daily

AFTER DARK

Mango's by the Sea £££ ❹   Set on the verandah of a colonial-style home, Mango's is a quaint hideaway with a reputation for fresh seafood dishes and warm, friendly service. ⓐ 2 West End, Queen Street, Speightstown ❶ 422 0704 Ⓦ www.mangosbythesea.com ❷ 18.00–21.45 daily

Mannie's Suga Suga Beach Bar £££ ❺   Mannie's is one of the most popular bars on the west coast, offering all-day dining, with a mixture of traditional Caribbean cuisine and Asian-fusion dishes. You can dine on its generous verandah facing the ocean or you can be served while lounging under a beach umbrella. ⓐ Mullins Bay ❶ 419 4511 ❷ 08.00–23.00 Mon–Wed, Fri & Sat, 08.00–19.00 Thur & Sun

◯ *Fisherman's Pub is a popular choice with locals and tourists alike*

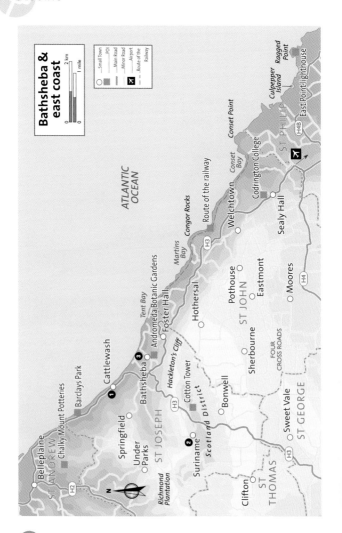

Bathsheba & east coast

ATLANTIC OCEAN

Bathsheba & east coast

Bathsheba is a quiet and charming fishing village on the rugged Atlantic coast of Barbados. It's a magnet for surfers and others who seek relaxation away from the whirl of activity on the south and west coasts. It is absolutely captivating: a wide swathe of golden sand flanked by gigantic boulders, and the sea touching the shore in wild waves driven by the ceaseless breeze. The water here is rough with strong undercurrents and it's not safe for swimming, but visitors (mostly locals) come to breathe in the fresh air, splash and cool off in the invigorating rock pools and feel refreshed. The 'Soup Bowl' as the bay at Bathsheba is called, is the surfing capital of the island and several competitions are held here annually – the Soup Bowl Café in the village is the centre of the surfing activity.

BEACHES

Tent Bay is a picturesque fishing area south of Bathsheba and Cattlewash. As on the other stretches of beach along this coast, swimming is not advisable because of strong currents. One of the landmarks is the Atlantis Hotel (being refurbished at time of writing), which has traditionally been a good spot to stop for lunch. South of Tent Bay is the small fishing village of **Martins Bay**, which has a shallow reef and many rock pools, and is known for the quality of the lobster caught there. **Bathsheba** has the safest and one of the most popular beaches on the east coast of the island. Framed by casuarina trees and very pleasant, it's a favourite picnic spot for families. There's a large car park, public toilets and changing rooms. The area was once a thriving sugar plantation.

THINGS TO SEE & DO

Andromeda Botanic Gardens
A lush garden with hundreds of varieties of tropical flowers, shrubs and trees, Andromeda was begun in 1954 as the project of local

◆ *Lush vegetation at Andromeda Botanic Gardens*

horticulturalist the late Iris Bannochie. She bequeathed the garden to the Barbados National Trust, which has continued her work. There's a stream running though the area as well as waterfalls and pools, and from the gardens are dramatic views of the east coast.

ⓐ Bathsheba ❶ 433 9384 ⏱ 09.00–17.00 daily ❶ Admission charge

Barclays Park

Queen Elizabeth II opened this expansive park in 1966, the year Barbados gained its independence from Britain; it was a gift from Barclays Bank International to mark the occasion. The park is on hilly land overlooking the scenic Cattlewash area, where the Atlantic waves pound the shores. The seaside picnic area is very popular, especially at weekends and public holidays. Barclays Park is the venue for the Party Monarch calypso competition, one of the big events of the annual Crop Over festival (see page 105).

Codrington College

Codrington College is the oldest Anglican theological college in the Western Hemisphere. It was built in 1743 with considerable funds and an estate bequeathed by Christopher Codrington. Many West Indian priests have trained at Codrington and the college continues to play an active part in education and theology. Perched high on a hill overlooking the Atlantic, it offers one of the most spectacular views of the east coast of Barbados. Visitors can wander around the grounds and visit the chapel.

ⓐ College Island, St John ❶ 423 1140 ⓦ www.codrington.org

Cotton Tower

The Barbados Trust maintains this 19th-century signalling station at Bowling Alley Hill, one in a chain of stations set up by the British Army as part of its security system, to alert the army both to slave rebellions or enemy ships. It's named after Lady Caroline Cotton, daughter of the island's governor. The tower isn't open to the public, but it's a pleasant place to wander around and soak up the atmosphere.

❶ 426 2421

Ragged Point area

Ragged Point is the easternmost point of the island and the East Point lighthouse overlooks a wild coastline of limestone cliffs and pounding waves. On a clear day you can see all the way up the coast to the northern points of the island, such as Cove Bay and Pico Tenerife. Off the coast lies Culpepper Island, a tiny island that can be easily reached at low tide. The East Point lighthouse is one of four on the island, the others being located at South Point, Needham's Point and Harrison Point.
ⓐ North of Highway 5, off Highway 4B

Route of the railway

A railway once ran along the east coast as far as Belleplaine from 1883 until 1937. The path of the railway line, though a bit difficult in places, makes a good walking trail from Bathsheba to Conset Bay.

TAKING A BREAK

The Cove ££ ❶ Simple and delicious Bajan food, buffet style, makes the lunches at The Cove stand out. It doesn't hurt that the restaurant also serves a mean rum punch and has breathtaking views of the idyllic Cattlewash beach. ⓐ Atlantic Park, Cattlewash ❶ 433 9495
🕒 12.00–15.00 Wed, Thur, Sat & Sun, closed Mon, Tues & Fri

Naniki ££ ❷ Set on a hillside with views of the ocean in the distance, Naniki has an out-of-the-way charm as well as an excellent Caribbean menu. ⓐ Lush Life Nature Resort, Suriname ❶ 433 1300
🌐 www.lushlife.bb 📧 info@lushlife.bb 🕒 12.30–15.30 Tues–Sun, closed Mon

Round House Inn ££ ❸ With a wonderful view of the Soup Bowl and its surfers, and its fortifying Bajan cuisine, the Round House has been a cherished east coast canteen for many years. ⓐ Bathsheba ❶ 433 9678
🌐 www.roundhousebarbados.com 🕒 08.00–22.00 Mon–Sat, 08.30–16.00 Sun

◆ *Boulders and waves at Bathsheba*

Crane Bay & southeast coast

Even though the southeast of Barbados has two of the loveliest beaches in Barbados (Crane Beach and Bottom Bay) and is not very far from the airport, the area hasn't attracted much tourist development. This is because, like other parts of this rugged coast, it is not generally good for swimming because of rough seas and strong undercurrents. The coast is, however, full of dramatic scenery, with long cliffs and rocky indentations interrupted by a few beaches, making it a treat for sightseers. There are also a few attractions well worth a visit, including one of the oldest rum distilleries and a plantation house over 300 years old.

BEACHES

Foul Bay is about 4 km (2½ miles) northeast of the airport and is the largest beach in this area. The road from the tiny village of Rices goes down to the beach, a long stretch of white sand with cliffs nearby. It's usually secluded, though there are often fishermen's boats resting on the sand. For an astonishingly beautiful bay, head a little further northeast to **Crane Beach**. Once a port, it was named after a huge crane that used to be used for loading and unloading ships. The Crane Resort, built on the cliff in 1867 and the first hotel on the island, has an imposing view of the gorgeous beach of pink sand. No wonder Crane Beach has been named one of the 'ten best beaches in the world' by *Lifestyles of the Rich and Famous*. There is a public access route to the beach but The Crane also allows access through the resort for a small fee, and it's worth it just to gaze upon the spectacular view from up there or even stay for lunch or drinks. Further east, just beyond Harrismith Beach is the beautiful pink-sand cove that is **Bottom Bay**. It's surrounded by high cliffs and is usually deserted, even in high season. Local families come here and tourists sometimes find this pleasant secret of a beach, but it's definitely off the beaten track.

⬤ View of the rugged coast from The Crane

THINGS TO SEE & DO

Foursquare Rum Factory and Heritage Park
The Foursquare Rum Factory is a state-of-the-art distillery built on the site of one of the oldest sugar estates in Barbados. The plantation was established in the 1640s during the earliest era of sugar cultivation on the island. The Heritage Park on the estate features an art gallery housed in a 250-year-old foundry of pink limestone, craft studios and a children's play area, as well as refreshment booths.

ⓐ South of Six Cross Roads, St Philip ⓣ 420 1977 ⓒ 09.00–16.00 Mon–Fri
ⓘ Free entry to park, but admission charge for optional tour of factory

Harrismith Great House
On the coast beyond Sam Lord's Castle is Harrismith Beach, and looming over it the old Harrismith Great House, once a hotel but now deserted and a bit spooky. There are steps just west of the house leading down from a cliff. It's beautiful and usually very quiet here, with palm trees, cliffs and small caves to explore.

Sunbury Plantation House
A fascinating journey into the past, this former plantation house has a wonderful collection of antique furniture, clothing, dolls, fine china, personal photos and farm equipment. This is the only plantation house in Barbados where all the rooms are open to visitors. There's a restaurant and bar, and on special nights a candlelit plantation dinner is set up at a beautiful 200-year-old table. The only missing piece is there's not a trace of the African slaves who would have toiled here.

ⓐ Northwest of Six Cross Roads, St Philip ⓣ 423 6270
ⓦ www.barbadosgreathouse.com ⓒ 09.00–17.00 daily (last tour 16.30)

TAKING A BREAK

Cutters of Barbados £ Combination gourmet deli and general store, Cutters offers sandwiches, pizzas, fine wines, beers, smoothies and their

▲ The idyllic Bottom Bay is off the beaten track

own special rum punch. It's right around the corner from The Crane Resort and almost impossible to miss, painted as it is in bright yellow. Offers take-away or breakfast and lunch on the verandah. ⓐ Cutters Building, St Philip ⓣ 423 0611 ⓦ www.cuttersbarbados.com ⓛ 08.30–18.30, closed Tues

L'Azure £££ An exquisite Caribbean seafood menu, plus other delectable dishes and a children's menu make L'Azure a favourite for a romantic dinner, executive lunch or special family outing. The warm but impeccable service and wonderful view of Crane Beach are added treats. ⓐ The Crane Resort, Crane Bay, St Philip ⓣ 423 6220 ⓦ www.thecrane.com ⓔ info@thecrane.com ⓛ 09.30–22.00 daily

Zen £££ This elegant restaurant is one of the most highly rated on the island for its heavenly Thai and Japanese dishes (including great sushi). A glass wall affords patrons views of the dramatic ocean below. ⓐ The Crane Resort, Crane Bay, St Philip ⓣ 423 6220 ⓦ www.thecrane.com ⓔ info@thecrane.com ⓛ 18.00–21.00 daily

ⓞ *Exotic residents of Orchid World*

EXCURSIONS
Out & about

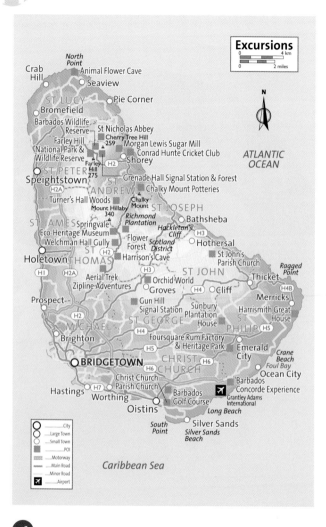

The northern tip

The northern tip of Barbados, encompassing the parish of St Lucy and a section of St Peter and St Andrew, is worlds away from the action further south and is the least visited part of the island. There aren't any hotels and restaurants here, but it's more than worth a day trip because of the many places of interest including a scenic park in the grounds of a ruined great house, a wildlife reserve where some of the residents leave in the morning and return in the afternoon, and one of the oldest houses in the English-speaking Caribbean.

GETTING AROUND

Organised tours from hotels make it easy to get to see all the attractions but for flexibility the best way to get around is by renting a car. There are buses that run from Speightstown to Bathsheba along Highway 2 past several places of interest, but they only run once an hour. The Barbados Transport Board also holds scenic Sunday tours, which are a good way not only to see the country but to enjoy some Bajan culture, as these excursions are popular with local people. Pack a picnic because there aren't many places to buy lunch.

THINGS TO SEE & DO

Animal Flower Cave

There aren't many sea anemones and tube worms left in the cave named after them ('animal flowers'), but there are other reasons to visit this intriguing cave at the rugged northernmost tip of the island. Created thousands of years ago by the sea, the cave has great rock pools for swimming and wonderful views out to sea.

ⓐ North Point, St Lucy ❶ 439 8797 ❷ 09.00–16.00 daily ❸ Admission charge. Inaccessible at high tide so call before you go

◆ *Sweeping views over the ocean from Cherry Tree Hill*

Barbados Wildlife Reserve

Originally established in 1985 for the conservation of the local green monkeys, the Barbados Wildlife Reserve was soon opened up as a tourist attraction. Visitors can stroll among the natural surroundings and get a close look at indigenous and non-native species of animals, many of them roaming free. There are tortoises, iguanas, snakes and small forest birds, as well as pelicans, peacocks and parrots, deer and caimans. The monkeys are undoubtedly the stars of the show, though, and they have free run of the area, leaving the reserve in the morning to roam among the trees of the forested area next to the reserve and returning in the afternoon for their 14.00 feeding – the best time to see them.

ⓐ Farley Hill, just north of Highway 2, St Andrew ⓣ 422 8826
ⓛ 10.00–17.00 daily ❶ Admission charge also allows entrance to nearby Grenade Hall

Cherry Tree Hill

North of the Morgan Lewis Sugar Mill (see page 80), through sugar cane lands and uphill, is this area of mature mahogany trees. Cherry Tree Hill is 259 m (850 ft) above sea level and offers stunning views of the Scotland District and out to the Atlantic Ocean. Local folklore says it got its name because cherry trees were once planted in the area but no one has proof of this.

Farley Hill National Park & Wildlife Reserve

The grounds of the once-majestic Farley Hill House, now in ruins and partially hidden away in a mahogany grove, are a favourite picnic spot for families and for weddings. It has spectacular views over the Scotland district and fresh, healthy breezes. The mansion was built in the 1800s and was used as a set in the 1957 movie *Island In The Sun* starring Harry Belafonte, but was later destroyed by fire. Farley Hill is also the venue for the annual Barbados Jazz Festival (see page 104).

ⓐ Farley Hill, St Peter ⓣ 422 3555 ⓛ 07.00–18.00 daily
❶ Admission charge per vehicle

Grenade Hall Signal Station & Forest

The Grenade Hall Signal Station was one of a series of communication towers built in the 19th century that were meant to notify the British garrison in Bridgetown of any slave uprisings on the island, and later of any suspicious foreign vessels lurking offshore. The watchtower affords a panoramic view of the area, and inside the station there are prints and some mementos from the British military and men who were stationed there. You're likely to see at least a few of Barbados' famous green monkeys scampering around the area as they leave the wildlife reserve nearby and forage among the trees in the cool shade of Grenade Hall Forest.

ⓐ Farley Hill, St Andrew ❶ 422 8826 ❶ Admission charge also allows entrance to the Barbados Wildlife Reserve

Morgan Lewis Sugar Mill

There were once more than 500 windmills on the island and though many still dot the landscape of the sugar lands, the Morgan Lewis Sugar Mill is the only one that still works. It's no longer used commercially but rather as a demonstration for visitors of the process of milling the sugar canes. There's an exhibition on the history of the island's windmills and a video on the milling process.

ⓐ Morgan Lewis, St Andrew ❶ 426 2421 ❶ 09.00–17.00 Mon–Sat
❶ Admission charge. Open one Sun a month for a live demonstration

St Nicholas Abbey

West of Cherry Tree Hill is the oldest house in Barbados and one of only three remaining Jacobean mansions in the Americas. It was built in around 1650 and was owned by very wealthy sugar growers. Despite its name, it has never been an abbey.

ⓐ Cherry Tree Hill, St Andrew ❶ 422 5357 ⓦ www.stnicholasabbey.com
ⓔ heritagetourism@stnicholasabbey.com ❶ 10.00–15.30 Sun–Fri, closed Sat ❶ Admission charge

🔺 *Morgan Lewis Sugar Mill is the last working mill on the island*

The east coast

Bathsheba, the surfing capital of Barbados, is the main attraction on the east coast, but there are many other surprises on this side of the island, both on the coast and inland. The scenic coast, with its craggy outline and wild seas, is a treat for the eye, and a drive to the area, perhaps with a stop for lunch or a stroll, makes for an invigorating day out.

GETTING AROUND

Organised tours from hotels make it easy to get to see all the attractions but for flexibility the best way to get around is by renting a car. There are public buses that leave from Bridgetown's River Bus Terminal; let the driver know beforehand where you want to be dropped off.

⬤ *The interior of St John's Church*

THINGS TO SEE & DO

Conrad Hunte Cricket Club

This is the island's most remote cricket pitch, situated as it is in the tiny village of Shorey near the northeast coast. Named after one of Barbados' greatest cricketers, the pitch boasts a spectacular view of the Atlantic Ocean on one side. Nearby are the villages of Belleplaine where the old railroad from Bridgetown ended, and Cattlewash, which got its name from the local custom of taking cows to the sea to bathe.

Hackleton's Cliff

For one of the best views of the east coast take a drive north from St John's Parish Church to Hackleton's Cliff. This steep escarpment marks the southern edge of the Scotland District and is the spot where it is believed a man named Hackleton committed suicide by riding his horse off the cliff.

St John's Parish Church

St John's Parish Church is a classic Gothic-style church, built in 1836, and perched on a cliff overlooking the picturesque east coast. In the

FORMATION OF THE SCOTLAND DISTRICT

The Scotland District comprises about 20 per cent of the island of Barbados. Although diminutive by comparison to some of the volcanic mountains in other Caribbean islands, Mount Hillaby, and with it the Scotland District, is the summit of an ancient underwater mountain range that extends several hundred kilometres from Trinidad in the south just about all the way to Puerto Rico. The Scotland District is the only place in the entire Caribbean where this mountain range is above water. Some of the rock formations here are 30 to 50 million years old.

churchyard cemetery lie the remains of Ferdinando Paleologus, a descendant of Emperor Constantine the Great, whose family was driven from the throne of Constantinople by the Turks. Ferdinando died in Barbados in 1678, after living on the island for over 20 years.

Near Hackleton's Cliff, St John 433 5599

Scotland District
The Scotland District is located in the east-central parishes of St Andrew and St Joseph. This hilly region of sheer cliffs and thick, forested areas was so named by Scotsmen homesick for their beloved Highlands, and is very different from most of the island. **Mount Hillaby** is the highest point in Barbados, at 340 m (1,116 ft) above sea level.

The central area

Many visitors to Barbados do not venture beyond the comfort of the major resort areas, but those who do discover the varied landscapes of this surprisingly diverse island. The central parishes of St Thomas and St George are quiet and the land here is flat and ideal for the sugar cane that was first planted here centuries ago and which is still being successfully cultivated. Further north, in St Andrew and St Joseph, is the island's most popular tourist attraction, Harrison's Cave and one of the island's newest adventure trails, the exciting Aerial Trek.

GETTING AROUND

Organised tours from hotels make it easy to get to see all the attractions but for flexibility the best way to get around is by renting a car. The Shorey village bus leaves from Bridgetown's Princess Alice Bus Terminal every hour and passes many of the sights in this area.

THINGS TO SEE & DO

Aerial Trek Zipline Adventures

This is a bracing, high adrenalin adventure in one of Barbados' forested gullies. Expert – and very reassuring – guides explain the safety procedures and the technique before they put you in a harness attached to a double row of ziplines and set you off among the treetops. They go along with you as you touch down at several platforms and give you some insights into the verdant world that surrounds you.

ⓐ Walkes Spring Plantation, Jack-in-the-Box Gully ❶ 433 8966
ⓦ www.aerialtrek.com ❶ 09.30–14.30 daily
❶ Admission charge. Min. age 12 yrs, max. weight 113 kg (250 lb/17½ st)

Chalky Mount Potteries

Chalky Mount is a high point in the area and is a short walk east of the village of the same name. The area is known as a good source of red clay

and there's a small community of potters in the village. You can see the artisans making mugs, pots, jugs and other items out of the local clay.

ⓐ Off Highway 2 near the Barclays Park area

Flower Forest

Three minutes' drive from Harrison's Cave, these beautifully landscaped botanic gardens are brimming with tropical blossoms, fruit and other indigenous trees and it's also home to the Barbados green monkey. There are wonderful views of the east coast and Mount Hillaby, the highest peak on the island.

ⓐ Richmond Plantation ☎ 433 8152 ⓔ ffl@sunbeach.net
🕐 09.00–17.00 daily ❶ Admission charge

Gun Hill Signal Station

You can see all of Barbados from the top floor of this fine signal station, built in 1818 as part of a security network. The restored station has an exhibition of military memorabilia and other artefacts, including one of

🔺 The white lion of Gun Hill Signal Station

HARRISON'S CAVE

This intricate system of limestone caves is located near the geographical centre of the island. The caves were first mentioned in historical documents in 1795 but it took nearly 200 years for them to be rediscovered and explored by Ole Sorensen, a Danish speleologist, and Barbadian Tony Mason. Sorenson had been commissioned by the Barbados National Trust and after surveying the cave, he recommended it be landscaped and developed as a tourist attraction. After several years of work digging tunnels, designing lighting and diverting underground streams, the Trust opened the cave to the public in 1981. Another major development was underway at the time of writing that will see the addition of a new visitor centre and interactive audio-visual area, a parking lot and elevators down to the starting point for the tour.

the island's earliest telephone directories. There's a massive white coral lion sculpture at the base of the hill that was carved from a single rock by an officer stationed here in 1868.

ⓐ Gun Hill, St George ❶ 429 1358 ❶ Admission charge

Harrison's Cave

There aren't enough superlatives to describe Harrison's Cave, the astonishing system of subterranean caves that is Barbados' most popular tourist attraction. After being shown a short video on the fascinating geological history of the cave and its development, visitors are taken on a tram ride that makes stops at two points in this eerie world of stalactites, stalagmites, pristine pools and the unparalleled Great Hall, acknowledged as one of the finest examples of cave architecture in the world.

ⓐ Welchman Hall, St Thomas ❶ 438 6640 ⓦ www.harrisonscave.com
ⓔ reservations@harrisonscave.com ❶ 09.30–16.00 Wed–Sun
❶ Admission charge

Orchid World

Thousands of varieties of orchids (not native to Barbados) are cultivated on this large, former farm. Visitors can walk along winding paths with orchids of every size, shape and colour basking in the open countryside and shaded areas on either side, and there are benches to sit and contemplate all this beauty.

ⓐ Groves, St George ☎ 433 0306 🕒 09.00–17.00 daily ❶ Admission charge

Springvale Eco-Heritage Museum

Springvale is a cultural museum showing rural life in Barbados as it was in times gone by. The museum is a former sugar plantation and there's an information centre as well as a café.

ⓐ Highway 2, St Andrew ☎ 438 7011 ⓔ newden@sunbeach.net
🕒 10.00–16.00 Mon–Sat ❶ Admission charge

Turner's Hall Woods

This is one of the last remnants of the dense tropical rainforest that covered Barbados when the first English settlers arrived in 1627, most of which was cleared for cultivation. The woods contain fine specimens of trees such as the sand box, silk cotton, fustic, cabbage palm, trumpet tree, locust and macaw palm. There are many green monkeys here as well and it's a good place for a hike – the trail goes uphill gradually to a great spot overlooking the sea on the rugged east coast of the island.

ⓐ West of Highway 2, St Andrew

Welchman Hall Gully

The forested Welchman Hall Gully is a collapsed extension of Harrison's Cave. It's beautiful for either cool, relaxing strolls or for more vigorous hiking. There are small caves, quite a bit of wildlife and a variety of trees and plants, including some towering palms. Pack a picnic lunch and linger a bit.

ⓐ Welchman Hall, St Thomas ☎ 438 6671
ⓦ www.welchmanhallgullybarbados.com 🕒 09.00–17.00 daily
❶ Admission charge

◆ *Harrison's Cave is a must-see*

EXCURSIONS

The south coast

Although it is one of two main centres of tourist development on the island, the south coast parish of Christ Church nevertheless has pockets where there are very few hotels and restaurants.

GETTING AROUND

It's cheap and easy to get around the southern part of the island with loads of buses and taxis (minibuses and cars) travelling the main road (Highway 7) in the heavily developed areas. You can catch a minibus anywhere along the route or at the Fairchild Street Bus Terminal in Bridgetown. Otherwise, rent a car and do your own driving.

THINGS TO SEE & DO

Christ Church Parish Church

An attractive and interesting church of coral stone, which is best known for the weird and true story of the Chase family tomb. On three occasions during the 19th century, when the tomb was opened for an internment it was found that the lead coffins inside were not in the same positions as before. When this happened a fourth time – after being locked by the governor's seal – the coffins were all taken out and buried in the churchyard.

ⓐ Church Hill, east of Oistins, where Highway 7 goes inland at Highway 6 ⓛ 09.00–17.00 daily

Oistins

Oistins is the main town in Christ Church and this large fishing village is quite busy by day, with fishermen bringing in their catch and preparing the fish for sale at the market. At night (especially on Fridays and Saturdays) its population expands as locals and visitors gather for its popular Fish Fry. In March the annual Oistins Fish Festival takes place, which is a bigger version of what takes place every weekend – lots of

⏷ *An evening out at the popular Fish Fry of Oistins*

delicious fried and grilled fish and other seafood to snack on, drinks flowing, a great 'lime' full of good-natured 'ole talk' and dancing to 'back-in-time' music. Even though the place has changed quite a lot and can be very crowded, this is a scene not to be missed.

SCENIC SUNDAYS FROM THE BARBADOS TRANSPORT BOARD

The Sunday Scenic Tours take passengers by bus to various sights around the island, rotating every month according to the week:

Week 1: Folkestone Park–Farley Hill–East Coast Road.

Week 2: Cherry Tree Hill–Little Bay–River Bay

Week 3: Foul Bay–Three Houses Park–Bath

Week 4: Bathsheba–King George V Park–Silver Sands

Buses leave Independence Square at 14.00 each Sunday and tickets are available at the Fairchild Street and Princess Alice Terminals, and the Transport Board headquarters, all in Bridgetown.

◗ *A rum shop by the beach*

Food & drink

The seas around Barbados yield a great variety of fresh fish and seafood, definitely the top choices on any menu. Fresh fish is sold daily at Oistins (see page 92) on the south coast and in other fishing villages, as well as in Bridgetown. It's fascinating to visit Oistins in the evening when the boats come in, even if you're not planning to buy fish, just to see all the activity involved in bringing in the catch, cleaning and selling the fish. Flying fish are a national emblem. Schools of these small fish shoot across the surface of the sea and drop back in (they don't actually 'fly'). When filleted and fried or baked, and accompanied by cornmeal cou-cou, you have the Barbadian national dish. Other types of fish are delicious too, especially red snapper, king fish and dolphin-fish (*mahi mahi* or

● *Barbados' drink of choice is, of course, rum*

dorado, *not* the mammal). Succulent shrimp and lobster are also good, if expensive, choices, and find their way on to plates at the most expensive restaurants, but also at regular grill joints and barbecues on the beach. Conch fritters and crab cakes are other local seafood favourites, and the roe of the white sea urchin, called 'sea eggs', while not always available, is delicious and worth a try if the opportunity arises.

Bajans's favourite meat is pork and it is often served in spicy stews or baked for Sunday lunch. While chicken is more of an everyday staple, lamb, beef, turkey, veal, duck and rabbit are also popular on the table.

Barbados' colonial history has imparted a definite British flavour to some aspects of its national cuisine: for example, many restaurants serve formal afternoon tea, and Jug Jug (a type of black pudding) is believed to have its origins in the haggis prepared by early Scottish settlers. However, the strongest influence on Barbadian food has been the majority African population. Ingredients commonly used like okra, plantains, sweet potatoes and other starchy vegetables have their origins in West Africa. Some of the foods given to slaves as rations, for example salted cod from Canada and breadfruit, originally brought from the South Pacific, now also form a cherished part of the local repertoire.

Like many other Caribbean islanders, Bajans have included some of the region's signature dishes among their own specialties. Trinidadian 'roti', with its spicy curried meats and vegetables, Jamaican 'jerk', peppery barbecued meat flavoured with pimento (allspice), and the long-simmering Guyanese 'pepperpot' ('cohobblopot' in Barbados) are three such adopted dishes.

There are several fast food franchises in Barbados but the island also has a home-grown version. Chefette (www.chefette.com) has many outlets all over the island that offer not only chicken and chips, burgers and pizza, but also serves rotis, wraps and has a great salad bar.

TRADITIONAL BAJAN DISHES
Cou-cou and flying fish Barbados' national dish combines tasty, fried flying fish and a polenta-like pudding made of cornmeal and ochroes

(okra). Cou-cou can also be made from breadfruit or green banana and can accompany spicy salt fish stews.

Pudding and souse Black pudding made with sweet potatoes and Bajan seasonings and accompanied by pickled pork is a Saturday favourite.

Saltfish Dried, salted cod is soaked and softened and made into fritters or fish cakes.

Jug-jug A stew made from corned beef, pork, pigeon peas and corn, usually prepared at Christmas.

Cohobblopot Known in most places as 'pepperpot', this dish is made from various types of meat, cooked with spicy seasonings. The crucial ingredient is casareep, an Amerindian flavouring and natural preservative which allows the stew to last for a long time, so a large cohobblopot can be made and be reheated over a number of days.

Cutters Bajan sandwiches made of meat on coconut bread and served mainly in small eateries, bars and rum shops.

Macaroni pie Simply known as 'pie' by Bajans, this is a staple side dish of the big Sunday lunch, made mainly with macaroni and cheese.

Conkies Pumpkin, sweet potato, cornmeal and coconut oil are mixed together and steamed in banana leaves to make a delicious pudding.

VEGETARIANS

The food markets in Barbados spill over with fresh fruit and vegetables of all kinds, yet vegetarians have to work harder than other people to get satisfaction. Some dishes that appear to be vegetarian, peas and rice for example, may be flavoured with salt pork or beef. However, things are improving and it is easier now to get strictly vegetarian food: there are a couple vegetarian restaurants and many others that now offer vegan and vegetarian dishes that are not just side orders, and Indian restaurants tend to have a wide selection of spicy, vegetarian dishes.

DESSERTS

Anyone with a sweet tooth will have no shortage of local treats to sample in Barbados. Sweet bread (heavy with fruits and coconut), sugar cakes (made with sweetened coconut and spices), guava cheese (which is similar to Turkish Delight), and a moist cassava dessert called cassava pone are among the most delicious. Local ice cream in flavours of coconut and ginger are simply irresistible, and Bajan black cake (a rich fruit cake spiked with lots of rum) is the *pièce de résistance* at Christmas.

DRINKS

Barbados rum is among the best in the Caribbean and it's no wonder that it is the first choice of Bajans. The regular blends are used for rum-and-coke and other mixed drinks but the more expensive, special blends are sipped straight. Mount Gay (see page 20) and Foursquare Rum Factory (page 72) are the two main factories, and Malibu (page 20) makes a coconut rum which is mixed with pineapple juice for a sweet light drink. There are dozens of 'rum shops' all over the island and Bajans love to point out that there are as many rum shops as churches. They tend to be the domain of men but are great spots to take in some local atmosphere: they serve drinks and local pub food, and opinionated 'old talk' flows freely on topics ranging from cricket to politics and anything in between.

The local Banks beer is a light golden lager made from a blend of barley and hops and it is by far the most popular brew among Bajans.

Non-alcoholic drinks include wonderfully refreshing fresh local fruit juices, such as the incomparable June plum, as well as lime, tamarind, cherry and coconut 'water'. Soft drinks and bottled water are available everywhere, and the tap water is safe to drink.

BARBADIAN DRINKS

Sorrel A Christmas drink made by boiling the flowers of the bitter sorrel plant, adding spices and sweetening to perfection.

Mauby This drink, made from the bitter bark of a tree, isn't for everyone, but it is a refreshing and healthy drink and worth trying.

Ginger tea Ginger tea is a local cure for the common cold and is drunk ferociously hot.

Poncha crèma A type of eggnog that's a potent combination of dark rum, condensed milk, eggs, lime juice, bitters and nutmeg.

Shopping

Barbados is a shopper's paradise of duty-free shops, with department stores and chic shops and boutiques in Bridgetown and along the south and west coasts, and several malls. There is also a lively art and craft scene that produces interesting works for galleries.

You can find excellent, hand-made pottery at craft shops, for example the Pelican Craft Centre (pages 22–4) in Bridgetown, or you can buy directly from the potters' studios. Beachside craft booths offer T-shirts, beachwear, jewellery and every kind of souvenir imaginable. If you need food for self-catering, there are well-stocked supermarkets, smaller grocery shops and markets.

Duty-free

Bridgetown's big department stores on Broad Street offer the world's best luxury goods, typically at cheaper prices than you'd pay in Europe or the USA. Alcohol and tobacco, perfumes, cameras, watches and electronics, gold and silver jewellery, gems, crystal and china, sunglasses and resort wear are among the most sought-after items. There are several shops in Holetown and Speightstown on the west coast that carry high quality duty-free goods. Visitors must show their passports and return tickets and they are allowed to pay for and take their merchandise right away, or purchases can be delivered to the airport or seaport for you.

Cave Shepherd ⓐ Broad Street, Bridgetown ⓣ 431 2121
ⓦ www.caveshepherd.com ⓘ Also branches in Holetown, at the airport and cruise ship terminal

Da Costas Mall ⓐ Broad Street, Bridgetown ⓣ 430 4844

Shopping plazas

On the outskirts of Bridgetown is the Bayshore Complex, worth a stop for its many shops, and also Pelican Village (see page 22), which is a good option for local handicrafts, such as straw bags, wall hangings, batik, paintings, rum cakes and cigars. There are also several other shopping malls and plazas located outside Bridgetown, including the charming Chattel House Village (see page 50), and shopping areas in St Lawrence Gap and Holetown that sell souvenirs, gift items, clothing and local arts and crafts. The West Coast Mall at Holetown is the biggest mall on that coast, while Hastings Plaza, Quayside Centre and Shak Shak Complex offer a collection of shops on the south coast. Sheraton Centre, off the ABC Highway in Christ Church, is popular with Barbadians and has 70 stores, a food court and a cinema complex.

Supermarkets

If you are staying at an apartment, villa or hotel with kitchen facilities, you may choose to do some cooking yourself. Your hotel front desk can advise of the nearest shopping facilities but some of the more popular ones are:

South coast: Big B Supermarket, Worthing; Julie 'N Supermarket, Worthing

West coast: Jordan's Supermarket, Payne's Bay; Super Centre, Holetown; Esso AutoMart, Payne's Bay

⬤ *Hand-made baskets for sale at the Pelican Craft Centre*

Children

Barbados is a family-friendly destination and many hotels make a lot of effort to ensure young visitors are kept just as happy as their parents. Activities for children range from arts and crafts projects to scavenger hunts and nature discovery expeditions. A few hotels do not accept children under 12 or have restrictions during the high season, so be sure to check when you are booking your holiday. Many have special activities for children and offer childcare or babysitting services. Hotels usually have shallow baby-swimming pools for children and they make a nice change from the beach.

Many restaurants cater for young children and have special menus with child-friendly dishes in smaller portions. You will find even some of the most upmarket restaurants are welcoming to families with children.

Children can spend hours and hours at the beach and there are safe beaches in the west of the island and to some extent in the south. However, as much as the sun is to be enjoyed, it should also inspire caution. Your holiday can be ruined by sunburn and, of course, it is also a long-term health risk, so be sure to cover your children (and yourselves) with a high factor sunscreen, and even with that protection do not spend too much time in the sun, especially during the middle of the day – from 11.30 to about 14.30. Hats and cover-ups also provide some protection.

Many of Barbados' attractions are fun for both adults and children; among them are the fantastic caves and waterfalls at Harrison's Cave (see page 87) and the Barbados Museum in Bridgetown (see pages 15–16), which has a delightful children's section. Children will love the green monkeys at the Barbados Wildlife Reserve (see page 79) and the aquarium at Ocean Park (see page 39). **Atlantis Submarines** take you on a real submarine journey which is enthralling, although a bit pricey (around US$102 per adult, US$52 per child, US$82 per teenager). Children must be a minimum height of 0.9m (3ft). ⓐ The Shallow Draught, Bridgetown ⓣ 436 8929 ⓦ www.atlantisadventures.com/barbados.cfm ⓔ barbados@res.atlantisadventures.com
ⓘ Tour lasts 2 hrs 20 mins with 40 mins spent underwater.

◆ *Beaches and the sea will provide endless fun*

Sports and activities

There's loads to do in Barbados if you decide to peel yourself away from your hotel.

BOAT TOURS
Boat cruises are a great way to explore the offshore attractions of Barbados. Full-package cruises include lunch and refreshments, stops to beaches and reefs for snorkelling. Party cruises are raucous, fun-filled affairs.
Cool Runnings Catamaran Cruises ⓐ Carlisle Wharf, Hincks Street, Bridgetown ❶ 436 0911 Ⓦ www.coolrunningsbarbados.com
El Tigre Catamaran Cruises ⓐ Prior Park Terrace, Bridgetown ❶ 417 7245 Ⓦ www.eltigrecruises.com

CRICKET
Bridgetown's Kensington Oval is one of the cricketing world's legendary grounds. From February to May it hosts a series of Test matches, One-Day Internationals and Twenty20 matches. ⓐ Bridgetown north ❶ 436 1397

GOLF
Barbados has a selection of 9- and 18-hole golf courses that give golfers of all levels of expertise a chance to enjoy their game.
Barbados Golf Club ⓐ Durants, Christ Church ❶ 428 8463 Ⓦ www.barbadosgolfclub.com
Rockley Golf Course ⓐ Rockley, Christ Church ❶ 435 7873 Ⓦ www.rockleygolfclub.com
Sandy Lane ⓐ Sandy Lane, St James ❶ 444 2000 Ⓦ www.sandylane.com

HIKING
The **Barbados National Trust** (ⓐ Wildey House, Wildey, St Michael ❶ 426 2421) organises regular free hikes that are a great way to get to know the island and meet people. The hikes allow for varying levels of fitness. If you prefer to explore without a guide, be sure you don't walk alone, and take a good, detailed topographic map.

HORSERACING

Horseracing has taken place at the Garrison Savannah for over 150 years. There are three seasons of racing per year (Jan–Apr, May–Aug & Oct–Dec).

Barbados Turf Club Ⓦ www.barbadosturfclub.com Ⓛ Racing every other Sat from around 13.00–17.45

JEEP TOURS

Jeeps tours are a great way to experience the natural beauty of Barbados and have some rugged adventure at the same time.

Adventureland Tours Ⓐ Wotton Plantation, Christ Church Ⓣ 437 7423 Ⓦ www.adventurelandbarbados.com

Island Safari Ⓐ The Belle Estate, St Michael Ⓣ 429 5337 Ⓦ www.islandsafari.bb

SPORT FISHING

Barbados provides excellent opportunities for big game fishing, for marlin, sailfish, tuna, wahoo, dorado and king fish. Many companies offer half- or whole-day charters and often allow shared charters.

Barbados Game Fishing Association Ⓦ www.barbadosgamefishing.com

WATERSPORTS

There are good surfing and windsurfing conditions just about every day of the year. Bathsheba is the surfing capital of Barbados and its annual competitions attract professional surfers from all over the world. Beaches on the south are the best for windsurfing. Coral reefs around the island make for excellent snorkelling and scuba-diving, with the calm west and south coasts providing the best sites. There are many reputable dive companies offering PADI certification courses, guided dives and snorkelling excursions.

Eco Dive Barbados Ⓐ Mt Standfast, St James Ⓣ 243 5816 Ⓦ www.ecodivebarbados.com

Hightide Watersports Ⓐ Coral Reef Club, St James Ⓣ 432 0931 Ⓦ www.divehightide.com

Festivals and events

Barbados has many festivals and events throughout the year. The dates of some events change from year to year, so it's wise to check the tourist board website (Ⓦ www.barbados.org), which has a detailed calendar of events.

JANUARY
Barbados Jazz Festival Some of the biggest names in international jazz take part in this week-long music festival. Some events are held at the open-air venue of Farley Hill National Park, which is ideal for a day of picnicking and music. ❶ 429 2084
Ⓦ www.barbadosjazzfestival.org

FEBRUARY
Holetown Festival This commemorates the arrival of the first British settlers on 17 February 1627. The week-long festival begins with celebrations at the Holetown Monument and is a showcase for Barbadian culture and history.
Ⓦ www.holetownfestivalbarbados.com

Carib Beer Cup A round-robin cricket competition among teams from several Caribbean nations, the Carib Beer Cup is played in different territories from November to March. Kensington Oval is the Barbados venue. ❸ Bridgetown north ❶ 436 1397

MARCH
Holders Season This is one of the premier cultural festivals in the Caribbean, featuring opera, music and theatre, in the setting of the grounds of a magnificent 300-year-old plantation house. Luciano Pavarotti sang here and the high quality of the performances and the graceful setting draw people from all over the world to this glamorous celebration of the performing arts. ❸ Holders House, St James
❶ 432 6385 Ⓦ www.holders.net

Agrofest The Barbados Agricultural Society's annual exhibition is popular with families. Farmers, artisans and processors of agricultural products display their goods during a three-day show. There are tropical flowers, a petting zoo and a food court serving Bajan delicacies. ☎ 436 6683 @ agrofest@caribsurf.com

APRIL
Oistins Fish Festival The annual festival celebrates the bounty of the sea and the fishing village of Oistins on Barbados' south coast. There are boat races, fishing competitions, seaside booths serving fried fish and DJs playing music for the lively crowd.

MAY
Gospelfest This festival celebrating Christian spirituality attracts a host of Caribbean and international gospel singers and bands who perform to enthusiastic crowds. The style of music varies from traditional Southern US gospel to reggae, calypso, soul and jazz. ☎ 426 5128 Ⓦ www.barbadosgospelfest.com

Celtic Festival This festival of song, music and dance celebrates the Celtic heritage of some of Barbados' early settlers, and attracts Irish, Welsh and Scottish visitors as well as locals. Haggis Night, Highland games and a rugby tournament are regular highlights. ☎ 426 3387 @ celticruth@hotmail.com

JULY TO EARLY AUGUST
Crop Over Festival Originally Barbadians marked the successful ending of the year's sugar cane harvest – and a period of rest for slaves and, later, paid workers – with a period of celebration. Nowadays, Crop Over is a colourful carnival and the biggest cultural event of the year. A season of shows featuring the island's biggest soca stars culminates on Grand Kadooment Day in a huge party on the Spring Garden Highway, with brilliantly costumed masqueraders dancing to the latest soca anthems. ☎ 424 0909 Ⓦ www.barbados.org/cropover.htm

NOVEMBER

Independence Day Pro Classic Surfing Championships This event attracts professional surfers from all over the world to Bathsheba, for one of the most exciting surfing events in the Caribbean. ☎ 228 5117

National Independence Festival of Creative Arts Barbados celebrates the anniversary of its independence from Britain by showcasing the talent of its best singers, dancers and performers of many kinds in an island-wide competition. ☎ 424 0909 🌐 www.ncf.bb

DECEMBER

Barbados gets running on the first Sunday in December, with five races being held on that day: a marathon, half-marathon, 10 km (6 miles), 5 km (3 miles) and a children's walk. ☎ 427 2623 🌐 www.runbarbados.org

PUBLIC HOLIDAYS

1 January New Year's Day
21 January Errol Barrow Day
April (date variable) Good Friday
April (date variable) Easter Monday
28 April National Heroes Day
1 May Labour Day
May (date variable) Whit Monday (eighth Monday after Easter)
1 August Emancipation Day
First Monday in August Grand Kadooment Day
First Monday in October United Nations Day
30 November Independence Day
25 December Christmas Day
26 December Boxing Day

○ *The entrance to the well-equipped Accra Beach Hotel*

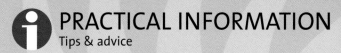

PRACTICAL INFORMATION
Tips & advice

Accommodation

The price guide is based on the cost of a double room for two people in the high season. During the low season, rates can reduce by up to around 25 per cent.

£ = BD$140–BD$320   ££ = BD$320–BD$500   £££ = more than BD$500

BATHSHEBA

Sea-U Guest House £ This friendly little guesthouse is surrounded by tropical gardens and faces the rugged Bathsheba coast. It's a very relaxing place, and the hammocks strung on the balconies of the rooms here attest to the laid-back vibe. ⓐ Tent Bay ⓣ 433 9450 ⓦ www.seaubarbados.com ⓔ sea-u@caribsurf.com

New Edgewater Hotel ££ A small oceanfront hotel at Bathsheba. There's a swimming pool and some rooms have private whirlpools. The hotel also has a business centre. ⓐ Bathsheba, St Joseph ⓣ 433 9900 ⓦ www.newedgewater.com

BRIDGETOWN & ENVIRONS

Island Inn Hotel ££ Once a rum storage facility for the British colonial regiment, the carefully restored building has been designated a Barbadian national treasure. Island Inn is known for its hospitality, Old World charm and great location at the Garrison historical area and also very near the beach. ⓐ Aquatic Gap, The Garrison ⓣ 436 6393 ⓦ www.islandinnbarbados.com

Hilton Barbados £££ A five-star hotel that dominates the peninsula of Needham's Point, the Hilton is surrounded by two white sand beaches and turquoise waters. Its location and services, including high-speed internet connection in guestrooms and meeting facilities, make it a good choice for business travellers, though holidaymakers are just as well served. ⓐ Needham's Point ⓣ 426 0200 ⓦ www.hiltoncaribbean.com

CRANE BAY

Crane Beach Resort and Residences £££ One of the oldest continuously operating resorts in the Caribbean, the Crane sits majestically on a cliff overlooking the ocean and one of Barbados' most spectacular and romantic beaches. There are five outdoor pools and two excellent restaurants at this upmarket but friendly resort. ⓐ Crane, St Philip ⓣ 423 6220 ⓦ www.thecrane.com

HASTINGS, ROCKLEY & WORTHING

Coconut Court Beach Hotel £ Friendly, family-run beachfront hotel with private balconies. There's live entertainment two nights a week, a pool, restaurant and beach bar overlooking a sheltered bay with a small reef. ⓐ The Garrison, Hastings ⓣ 427 1655 ⓦ www.coconut-court.com

Blue Orchids Beach Hotel ££ A family-friendly beachfront hotel that has been recently renovated and extended. Blue Orchids is an official partner of the Barbados Golf Club and offers special golf packages. The surrounding white beaches and gardens are excellent venues for weddings. ⓐ Highway 7, Worthing ⓣ 435 8057 ⓦ www.blueorchidsbarbados.com ⓔ blorchids@caribsurf.com

Sandy Bay Beach Club ££ A large, informal, all-inclusive hotel set on a lovely beach protected by a coral reef. Visitors can sometimes see marine turtles laying their eggs on the beach or swimming in the ocean. ⓐ Worthing ⓣ 435 8000 ⓦ www.sandybaybeachclub.com ⓔ vacation@sandybaybeachclub.com

Accra Beach Hotel and Resort £££ Set on the lively Rockley Beach, Accra is a favourite choice for beach-lovers, but is also a good bet for business clients. Features excellent conference facilities, its famous swim-up bar, Chakra Spa and the island's only Polynesian restaurant. ⓐ Highway 7, Rockley ⓣ 435 8920 ⓦ www.accrabeachhotel.com

The Savannah Hotel £££ This 200-year-old beachfront hotel is located near to Garrison Savannah, the historic horse-racing track. One of the two freshwater pools meanders the length of the new wing. This charming hotel is considered a great honeymoon destination.
ⓐ Hastings ① 435 9473 ⓦ www.gemsbarbados.com

HOLETOWN

The Sandpiper Hotel £££ An exclusive beachfront hotel set amid lush tropical gardens, the Sandpiper is a member of Condé Nast Johansens Small Luxury Hotels of the World. The Tree Top suites have private plunge pools. ⓐ Holetown, St James ① 422 2251 ⓦ www.sandpiperbarbados.com
ⓔ reception_group@sandpiperbarbados.com

Sandy Lane Hotel £££ One of the island's premier hotels favoured by international celebrities, Sandy Lane combines classical elegance with state-of-the-art facilities. There's a full range of watersports at the Beach Club and activities for children at the Tree House Club, plus superb restaurants and a spa offering the best in restorative treatments.
ⓐ St James ① 444 2000 ⓦ www.sandylane.com

Tamarind Cove Hotel £££ This romantic hotel on one of the island's loveliest beaches has a fully equipped business centre, two event rooms and three freshwater swimming pools, making it ideal for both business and pleasure. ⓐ Paynes Bay, St James ① 432 1332
ⓦ www.tamarindcovehotel.com

ST LAWRENCE GAP & DOVER
Peach and Quiet Hotel £ Unpretentious ocean-front hotel with fan-cooled bedrooms and the island's only sea rock pool. Winner of Travelers' Choice Award – Best Bargain in 2009. ⓐ Inch Marlowe ① 428 5682
ⓦ www.peachandquiet.com ⓔ res.peachandquiet@caribsurf.com

Dover Beach Hotel ££ A comfortable beachfront hotel located on the beautiful Dover Beach and also within easy walking distance of the

activity-filled St Lawrence Gap. **a** St Lawrence Gap **t** 428 8076
w www.doverbeach.com **e** vacation@doverbeach.com

Southern Palms Beach Club ££ A peaceful beachfront hotel just steps
from the bustling St Lawrence Gap. The hotel has a comprehensive
environment management system, is 'Green Certified' and actively
supports a carbon-offset programme. **a** St Lawrence Gap **t** 428 7171
w www.southernpalms.net **e** reservations@southernpalms.net

Little Arches Hotels £££ A stylish boutique hotel located next to
Enterprise Beach, Little Arches features Mediterranean-style architecture
and custom-made furniture, and is open to adults only. Its rooftop
restaurant, Café Luna, was rated in the top three of the Zagat 2008/2009
Survey in the categories of Best Food and Best Décor, among others.
a Enterprise Road (south of Oistins) **t** 420 4689
w www.littlearches.com **e** paradise@littlearches.com

SPEIGHTSTOWN
Angler Apartments £ These air-conditioned apartments (studio and
one bedroom) just across the road from a lovely beach are a good
deal for those who prefer to be self-catering. **a** Clarke's Road, Derricks
t 432 0817 **w** www.anglerapartments.com **e** info@anglerapartments.com

Almond Beach Village £££ This large, all-inclusive, beachfront hotel set
on a former sugar plantation has a lively mix of activities, including a
nine-hole golf course, squash and tennis courts as well as a nursery and
kids' club. **a** Heywoods, St Peter **t** 422 4900 **w** www.almondresorts.com

Cobblers Cove Hotel £££ Built in English Country House style and located
in a secluded setting, this hotel is a member of the exclusive Relais &
Châteaux organisation. Each of its 40 suites has its own living room and
balcony. **a** Speightstown, St Peter **t** 422 1460 **w** www.cobblerscove.com
e reservations@cobblerscove.com

Preparing to go

GETTING THERE

Most visitors arrive in Barbados by air. All flights (scheduled and charter) arrive at the Grantley Adams International Airport in the south of the island. There are daily non-stop, direct and indirect flights out of the United Kingdom, North America and other Caribbean islands to Barbados, and the route is serviced by many carriers including the following:

Air Canada ☎ 800 744 2472/428 5077 🌐 www.aircanada.com
American Airlines ☎ 800 433 7300/428 4170 🌐 www.aa.com
British Airways ☎ 800 247 9297 🌐 www.britishairways.com
Caribbean Airlines ☎ 800 744 2225/428 1650 🌐 www.bwee.com
LIAT ☎ 888 844 5428/428 8888 🌐 www.liatairline.com
SVG Air ☎ 800 744 5777 🌐 www.svgair.com
US Airways ☎ 800 428 4322 🌐 www.usairways.com
Virgin Atlantic ☎ 800 862 8621 🌐 www.virginatlantic.com

Many people are aware that air travel emits CO_2, which contributes to climate change. You may be interested in the possibility of lessening the environmental impact of your flight through the charity Climate Care, which offsets your CO_2 by funding environmental projects around the world. Visit 🌐 www.jpmorganclimatecare.com

Many visitors also arrive on cruise ship, yachts or by ferry from other islands. Ships dock at Bridgetown Harbour, and the Cruise Ship Terminal has a Barbados Tourism Authority office and duty-free shops. A tax of £4 is payable by each cruise ship passenger arriving at Bridgetown and those who arrive by yacht or ferry must register at the **Immigration Department** (ⓐ Careenage House, The Wharf, Bridgetown ☎ 426 1011) or they will have difficulty when leaving the island.

TRAVEL INSURANCE

Buying travel insurance is strongly recommended. There are excellent deals to be had if you shop around, ranging from short-break to annual cover. However, many of the basic options exclude certain activities, and if you are planning to go scuba diving or snorkelling, ride a motorbike or engage in other pastimes deemed higher risk, then you will almost certainly need to pay a little extra for coverage.

BARBADOS TOURISM AUTHORITY

The Barbados Tourism Authority (BTA) has several international offices that can provide information on the island prior to your trip. Visit the website (see below) to find out about entry formalities, accommodation, dining, activities and any other questions you may have. On the island, you can get information from the BTA's head office.

ⓐ Harbour Road, Bridgetown ⓣ 427 2623 ⓦ www.barbados.org
ⓔ btainfo@barbados.org

Tourist offices overseas

Canada Barbados Tourism Authority ⓐ Suite 1010,
105 Adelaide Street West, Toronto, Ontario M5H 1P9 ⓣ 416 214 9880
ⓦ www.barbados.org/canada ⓔ canada@barbados.org

UK Barbados Tourism Authority ⓐ 263 Tottenham Court Road, London
W1T 7LA ⓣ 020 7636 9448 ⓦ www.visitbarbados.co.uk
ⓔ btauk@visitbarbados.org.

USA Barbados Tourism Authority ⓐ 820 Second Avenue, 5th Floor,
New York, NY 10017 ⓣ 212 551 4350 ⓔ btany@barbados.org

BEFORE YOU LEAVE

No vaccinations are required for Barbados but it is wise to contact the Barbados Tourism Authority in your country for the most current information. It is also a good idea to make sure your tetanus and regular inoculations are up to date. There are many good pharmacies on the island, but bring any prescription drugs that you take regularly and a first-aid kit for any minor cuts and bruises. Make sure to pack a good supply of sunscreen, with an SPF of at least 30 – no matter what your skin colour, sunscreen is essential protection against the sun. Insect repellent is also a must in case of pesky mosquitoes, and it's advisable to wear lightweight long-sleeved shirts and long trousers as added protection in the evening. Generally, it's best to pack light, comfortable garments in natural fabrics and something elegant for dinner or going to clubs, along with your beachwear. Note that it is illegal (even for children) to wear camouflage clothing in Barbados, so no matter how comfortable or fashionable, please leave your camo kit at home.

🔺 *Go prepared and take plenty of sunscreen cream*

ENTRY FORMALITIES

Citizens of the UK, most Western European countries, the USA, Canada, Australia and Japan need a valid passport to enter Barbados, which must be valid for the duration of their trip; visas are not required for stays of up to six months. Citizens of Portugal, Sweden and Switzerland are limited to a stay of 28 days without a visa. Visas are required for citizens of the CIS, Eastern European countries, China, Taiwan, Pakistan, the non-Commonwealth countries of Africa, and all South American countries except Argentina, Brazil, Colombia and Venezuela.

Visas are not required for passengers on cruise ships, with the exception of citizens of the CIS, Eastern European countries, China, Taiwan, South Africa and Korea. Cruise ship passengers who are 'in-transit' and continuing on their cruises are not subject to immigration control and therefore not required to carry a valid passport. They may go ashore and return to their ship using their ship's magnetic identification card. However, cruise ship passengers whose trips begin and end in Barbados, or who are connecting to flights out of Grantley Adams International Airport, would need to show a valid passport. For more information on cruises and requirements, you can consult the Barbados Cruise Tourism website (Ⓦ www.cruisebarbados.com).

The fee for a single entry visa is BD$50 and for a multiple entry visa is BD$60. Visas may be obtained from any of Barbados' high commissions and embassies overseas.

MONEY

The Barbados dollar is tied to the US dollar at a rate of BD$2.00 to US$1.00. Most businesses accept either currency and major credit cards are widely accepted at hotels, restaurants and shops.

Banking hours are 09.00–15.00 Mon–Thur, 09.00–17.00 Fri. The Barbados National Bank at the airport is open every day from 08.00 until the last plane departs or arrives. There are also many ATMs across the island.

CLIMATE

Barbados has a tropical climate all the year round, with average temperatures between 24–29°C (75–84°F). The dry season, from December to April, is also the high season for tourism. The hurricane season is from June to November, but though the island has to be on hurricane watch from time to time, an actual hit is very rare. Visiting Barbados in the low season is cheaper and even in the rainy season the weather is still usually fine, with a shower or two during the day, usually at around lunchtime, leaving plenty of time to enjoy the sun.

BAGGAGE ALLOWANCE

Most airlines will allow you to travel with two checked bags of 23 kilos each, and a single piece of hand luggage; some allow a laptop bag or handbag as well. You can usually pay an excess charge for checked bags over 23 kilos, but few airlines will accept pieces that weigh more than 32 kilos for health and safety reasons. Continuing restrictions on liquids in hand luggage mean that you can only carry liquids or gels in containers of under 100 ml, and all liquids must be separated from the rest of your things in a clear zip-lock bag. As baggage allowances change frequently, however, it's best to treat the above information as a guideline only, and check with your airline before you travel.

During your stay

AIRPORTS

All flights coming in to Barbados touch down at the Grantley Adams International Airport which is about 16 km (10 miles) east of the capital, Bridgetown. Airport porters are usually tipped BD$2 per bag for transporting luggage to the street outside of the terminal. Facilities at the airport include a bank, bar, duty-free shops and a restaurant. Free public wireless internet access is available. There is a regular bus service (costing BD$1.50) to the city which departs every 10 minutes and takes 45 minutes. There is a 24-hour taxi service, and travel time to Bridgetown is 30 minutes. Be sure to find out from the driver what the cost of travel is before you begin your trip, as prices vary according to which part of the island you are going. You can also rent a car at the airport.

An airport service charge (formerly the departure tax) of BD$60 is automatically included in the cost of a ticket for all passengers over 12 years old leaving Barbados, so cash is no longer collected for this at the airport.

Grantley Adams International Airport ☎ 418 4242 Ⓦ www.gaiainc.bb

COMMUNICATIONS

Internet Barbados has excellent internet and related services and there are internet cafés with terminals and fast connections in all of the tourist centres. Many hotels, restaurants and bars also have wireless networks. Some places charge for wireless access but most have open networks which you can access for free.

Postal services There are 18 postal counters located across Barbados, including the General Post Office at Cheapside in Bridgetown and post offices at the Grantley Adams International Airport and the Bridgetown Cruise Terminal. There are also conveniently located red postboxes in walls, and cemented bins across the island. Express Mail Service (EMS), offering a more rapid service for either local or international mail, can be purchased from any district post office. Opening hours are variable, but as a general guide they are: 08.00–16.30 Mon–Fri at the main Bridgetown office; 07.30–12.00 & 13.00–15.00 Mon, 08.00–12.00 & 13.00–15.30 Tues–Fri at other branches.

Airmail postage rates for the first 10 grams are BD$1.75 for UK and Europe, and BD$1.40 for Canada and the USA.

Telephones Barbados has a dependable, island-wide telephone service. The phone system is linked to the United States DDD system and, therefore, direct credit card calls can be made. Visitors can bring their mobile phones and buy a local SIM card for use in their (unlocked) phones or rent one locally. Mobile phones can also be purchased from Cable & Wireless and Digicel. C&W and Digicel Barbados use the GSM standard. Roaming agreements exist with many international mobile phone companies and coverage is very good. (**Cable & Wireless** ❶ 800 804 2994; 292 2677. **Digicel** ❶ 434 3444)

Pay phones are widely available. BD$0.25 gives you a call approximately five minutes' long. Pay phones are identified by their blue shells and have Cable & Wireless written on them. Phonecards are available at most petrol stations, leading supermarkets and many stores in tourist areas.

TELEPHONING BARBADOS

The country code for Barbados is 246. To call the island from the UK, dial 001 followed by 246 and the seven-digit number. To call from the USA, dial 1 followed by 246 and the seven-digit number.

TELEPHONING ABROAD

To call the UK from Barbados, dial 011 followed by 44 for the UK, then the area code (minus the first zero) followed by the number. To call the USA from Barbados, dial 1 followed by the area code and number.

CUSTOMS

Barbadians are relaxed and sociable but at their core are conservative, church-going people. They do not generally appreciate public displays of lewd behaviour or excessive intimacy. They are generally polite people who greet one another with 'Good morning' or 'Good evening' and find it rude when visitors dispense with these social graces and just bluntly ask for what they want. Polite and respectful conduct on the part of visitors is usually rewarded with friendliness and good service.

DRESS CODES

In general wear clothes that keep you cool and protect you from the sun: choose garments that are casual and lightweight, in cotton or other natural fabrics. If you plan to go to religious services, the dress code is usually more formal attire and Sunday Mass all over the island is a 'dress-up' occasion.

Beachwear is acceptable at the beach but not in Bridgetown or other towns, as Barbadians are a conservative people and consider too much exposed flesh in public to be offensive. If you are staying near the beach, a cover-up should be worn when you are going from the beach to your hotel or taking a stroll in the town. Topless bathing in public is generally frowned upon but if you are staying at a hotel on a very secluded beach you could ask if it's permissible.

ELECTRICITY

Barbados runs on the system of 110 V/50 Hz. The island uses the North American-style 2-prong plug. Most 60 Hz appliances will work and many hotels provide a 220 V outlet in the bathrooms and adaptors.

EMERGENCIES
In case of emergency dial:
211 for the police
311 for the fire department.
511 Queen Elizabeth Hospital Ambulance Service

GETTING AROUND

Barbados is a highly navigable island and visitors have the choice of rental cars, public buses, taxis and motor scooters to get around. Driving is on the left side of the road. It is easy to know if you are going in the right direction as the road signs marking distance from Bridgetown helpfully say 'To City' or 'Out of City', but bear in mind there are many tiny roads veering off in all directions in rural areas and sometimes you may get lost. Take a detailed map, but if you get lost Bajans are usually very willing to give you directions to help you on your way.

Car hire You'll need a visitor's driving permit to rent a vehicle. The permit costs BD$100 and is available from any police station, car rental company

◗ Renting a car will give you great freedom

or at the airport rental agency, on presentation of a valid driving licence from your home country.

Other rentals It is also possible to rent motor scooters and bicycles, excellent for the adventurous and ecologically aware.

Public transport There is an efficient system of minibus taxis that radiate out from the hub of Bridgetown. This is how most Barbadians travel to and from work, and it's a cheap and good way to get around if you are not renting a car.

HEALTH, SAFETY AND CRIME
Barbados' water is filtered naturally by limestone and coral and pumped from underground streams. It is among the purest in the world and safe to drink. Standards of food hygiene are generally excellent, so there's no reason to avoid foods like salads, fruits, ice in drinks or ice cream.

Queen Elizabeth is the main public hospital on the island.
ⓐ Martinsdale Road, St Michael ❶ 436 6450
Bayview Hospital is one of the best private hospitals on the island.
ⓐ St Paul's Avenue, Bayville, St Michael ❶ 436 5446
All hotels would be able to recommend a dentist or doctor in the event of minor ailments.

If you are the victim of a crime, call the above numbers in an emergency, but bear in mind that response times can be slow depending on whether the police have available resources. The main police station is the Central Police Station.
ⓐ Coleridge Street, Bridgetown ❶ 430 7100

You can also contact the consular representative of your home country if you find yourself in distress.
British High Commission ❶ 436 6694
United States Embassy ❶ 436 4950
Canadian High Commission ❶ 429 3550

If you need medical help there are many private and public health facilities, the primary ones being the 600-bed Queen Elizabeth Hospital and the Bayview Hospital. There are also eight government polyclinics providing free medical attention for minor ailments, and dental treatment in some cases, along with many private medical and dental practitioners. A reciprocal health agreement with the UK entitles UK nationals to free hospital and polyclinic treatment and ambulance travel. There are numerous pharmacies and dental clinics. Private health care is quite expensive and serious cases that require specialist treatment may require emergency evacuation. There is also a very sophisticated decompression chamber on the island.

Barbados has a relatively low crime rate, but there is some petty theft, occasional muggings and there have also been a few high-profile violent crimes in recent years. Thus, while Barbados is one of the safest tourist destinations, visitors should still maintain the same level of personal security awareness as they do at home. Keep your valuables locked up in your hotel safe and be careful with your belongings when in public. It is wise for tourists to avoid high-risk activities such as walking on secluded beaches day or night, or in secluded areas away from main roads. If you are the victim of a crime, report it to the police. You may be offered drugs, but bear in mind that marijuana, cocaine and other narcotics are illegal in Barbados and carry heavy sentences, so do not get involved in this activity. And by no stretch of the imagination must you even consider smuggling drugs back home with you.

If you need help with directions or need assistance, look for a police officer to help. Members of the Royal Barbados Police Service are identifiable by their uniform: black trousers with a red stripe down the sides, grey, short-sleeved shirt with bars on the sleeves indicating rank, and a hat.

MEDIA

There are two privately owned daily newspapers, the *Nation* and the *Barbados Advocate*, and a mix of private and public radio stations as well as a lively blog presence. A bi-weekly regional paper, *Caribbean Week*, is also available island-wide. Two visitor publications, the *Visitor* and *Sunseeker*, come out every two weeks and are available free at most tourist outlets. The country's sole television station is run by the government-owned Caribbean Broadcasting Corporation (CBC). The CBC also operates MCTV, a multi-channel and pay-TV service. DirectTV is available on the island and most hotels provide international cable viewing.

OPENING HOURS

Opening hours for shops and businesses are generally 08.00–17.00 Mon–Fri and 08.00–16.00 Sat. Supermarkets are open later on Saturdays. Banks are open 08.00–15.00 Mon–Thur and 08.00–17.00 on Fri.

RELIGION

The majority of the population of Barbados are practising Christians, with the largest number of people being Anglicans. In all there are over 100 religious groups in Barbados, and other denominations include Roman Catholic, Methodist, Moravian, Spiritual Baptist, Seventh Day Adventist, Pentecostal, Rastafarian, Hindu and Muslim. Modest attire is the norm when entering places of worship.

SMOKING LAWS

Some restaurants have smoking and non-smoking sections, while others have smoke-free policies. Call ahead to make sure you will be comfortable, as a smoker or a non-smoker.

TIME DIFFERENCES

Barbados operates on Atlantic Standard Time, which is four hours behind the UK's Greenwich Mean Time, and one hour ahead of Eastern Standard Time in the USA.

TIPPING

Many restaurants include a service charge or tip (usually 10 per cent) on their bill but gratuity is normally at the discretion of the guest. At most restaurants and bars, tips are divided equally between all the staff, so

tips to a specific waiter should be given discreetly. It is common to add 10 per cent to taxi fares and tip porters at around BS$2 a bag.

TOILETS

Public toilets can be found in some of the larger establishments in Bridgetown as well as the malls outside of Bridgetown, including Cave Shepherd on Broad Street.

TOURIST INFORMATION

Barbados has an excellent tourism infrastructure, and maps, brochures and information about activities can easily be found at hotel reception areas and booths at the airport as well as at restaurants and shops around the island. The Barbados Tourism Authority website (Ⓦ www.barbados.org) is full of useful information for travellers and several free glossy tourist magazines are published regularly and are widely available. The Barbados Hotel and Tourism Association (Ⓐ 4th Avenue, Belleville, St Michael Ⓣ 426 5041 Ⓦ www.bhta.org) is also a good source of information.

TRAVELLERS WITH DISABILITIES

Some hotels and restaurants have wheelchair access and disabled toilets. The bigger hotels have lifts, and some hotels have rooms on the ground floor for people with disabilities or elderly people. When making plans for dining out or sightseeing it's best to call ahead and find out what's available.

People with disabilities can contact the National Disabilities Unit to find out what resources and support are available for their vacation.
National Disabilities Unit Ⓐ Hastings Towers, Christ Church Ⓣ 228 2978 Ⓔ natdisability@sunbeach.net

The Aquatic Centre in association with the Paralympics Association has a pool lift on location.
Aquatic Centre Ⓐ Sir Garfield Sobers Sports Complex, Wildey, St Michael Ⓣ 437 6010 Ⓦ www.gymnasiumltd.com.bb/html/aquatic.cfm